The Pastor's Playbook

The Pastor's Playbook

COACHING YOUR TEAM FOR MINISTRY

Stan Toler and Larry Gilbert

Beacon Hill Press of Kansas City
Kansas City, Missouri

SPECIAL THANKS

To Debra White Smith for editorial consultation and content review.

To Jerry Brecheisen, brother loved, for creative assistance and invaluable insight.

To the Beacon Hill Press team—Hardy Weathers, Kelly Gallagher, Bruce Nuffer, Bonnie Perry, Shannon Hill, and Michael Estep—for faith, confidence, and encouragement.

To Jim Buchan, Michelle Fain, and Derl Keefer for creative insight and assistance.

To Deloris Leonard for manuscript preparation and editorial guidance.

CONTENTS

ABOUT THE AUTHORS

Stan Toler is the pastor of Trinity Church of the Nazarene in Oklahoma City. He is the author of more than 30 books and manuals and hosts the television program *Leadership Today* on the Nazarene Communications Network. He resides with his wife, Linda, and their two sons in Bethany, Oklahoma.

Larry Gilbert is the founder, chairman, and CEO of the Church Growth Institute, through which he has published a number of books on team ministry, evangelism, and strategy. He also speaks on spiritual gifts and evangelism. He and his wife, Mary Lou, live in Elkton, Maryland.

INTRODUCTION

BASKETBALL GREAT MICHAEL JORDAN once scored a remarkable 64 points in a game against the Orlando Magic, but his team lost the game anyway. Even though Michael's scoring ability and dazzling acrobatics made him an instant superstar, he was in the NBA for six seasons before his team attained a championship. Jordan discovered that it wasn't very satisfying to be a superstar on a losing team. Being the NBA Rookie of the Year in 1985 was wonderful, and it was quite an achievement to be the top scorer in the league for seven consecutive seasons beginning in 1987, but Michael longed for an NBA championship.

He had to learn to direct his sensational abilities toward helping his team win, rather than merely scoring a lot of points. When he began to devote himself to teamwork—helping each of his teammates reach their full potential—the results were dramatic. Before his retirement from the game in 1999, Michael led the Chicago Bulls to six NBA championships.

> Individualism wins trophies, but teamwork wins championships.
>
> —Pat Riley

Church leaders need to learn the same lesson. Rather than striving for personal ministry "stardom" they need to develop ministry teams within their churches. The "team" concept is the foundational strategy for effective ministry in a local church.

The apostle Paul acknowledged that his ministry accomplishments were achieved with the help of many other people. Their love, encouragement, prayers, and financial support were indispensable to his success. (See 2 Cor. 1:11; 1 Cor. 16:17-18; Rom. 16:1-6; Phil. 2:19-30.) He didn't consider the people in his churches to be his "audience" but rather, his "fellow workers" (2 Cor. 1:24).

Paul, like Michael Jordan, was so gifted that he undoubtedly was tempted to "go it alone." The great apostle and the famous basketball player weren't in the same league (literally and figuratively), but they both understood that working together with others was the key to maximum success. They knew that the way to victory was more in their "assists"—providing others with opportunities to achieve—than in scoring their own points. They learned to see themselves not only as players but also as "coaches" who could bring out the gifts in their teammates.

> The main ingredient in stardom is the rest of the team.
> —John Wooden

The Bible doesn't emphasize *solo* ministry as much as it does *team* ministry. Its pages are filled with stories of great collaborations: Moses and Aaron, Caleb and Joshua, Esther and Mordecai, Ezra and Nehemiah, Peter and John, Paul and Timothy, Barnabas and Mark. Even the Gospels are presented to us by a team: Matthew, Mark, Luke, and John. Jesus made teamwork a priority in His earthly ministry with His team of 12.

Overworked church administrators can effectively utilize the skills of laypersons gifted by the Holy Spirit for ministry. Pastors can learn the dynamics of a "Ministry Action Team" philosophy that will revolutionize their local churches. Laypersons can gain insights into their own potential for leading their communities to Christ and for building His kingdom.

We pray that you can "get the job done" through gifted individuals who will catch your vision for changing the world. Discover the joys of working as a team for the glory of God.

Serving Christ and His Church,
Stan Toler and Larry Gilbert

1

Building Ministry Action Teams

Two are better than one, because they have a good reward for their labor. For if they fall, one will lift up his companion. But woe to him who is alone when he falls, for he has no one to help him up.

(Eccles. 4:9-10)

CHURCHES SHOULD BE MUCH MORE than Sunday morning "entertainment centers" for lukewarm saints. They should be "training centers" where people learn how to win the lost for Christ. They should be growing by adding souls to the Kingdom. But statistics show that only 20 percent of our churches are growing at all, and less than 5 percent are growing by conversions rather than transfer. This appalling lack of tangible results must call us to our knees in prayer and then to our feet in action if the church is to fulfill the Great Commission that our Lord entrusted to us. Failure to employ effective ministry teams could be a major cause.

Roberta Hestenes said in Fuller Theological Seminary's *The Pastor's Update,* "Many churches are structured for maintenance rather than for empowering ministry among all God's people. We must reexamine our structures so that the new can come into being while preserving the essentials of our faith."

Most pastors know in their hearts that they can't single-handedly win the lost. They know they must have the active participation of the entire church. Successful church leadership isn't about superstardom; it's about effective team building. Dedicated pastors have suffered burnout because they never learned this principle. Trying to do the job alone, they ended up much like the bricklayer who wrote the following letter to an insurance company to explain his injuries:

Dear Sir:

I am writing in response to your request for more information concerning block No. 11 on the insurance form, which asks for "Cause of Injuries," wherein I put "trying to do the job alone." You said you needed more information, so I trust the following will be sufficient:

I am a bricklayer by trade, and on the date of injuries I was working alone laying brick around the top of a four-story building, when suddenly I realized that I had about 500 pounds of brick left over. Rather than carry the bricks down by hand, I decided to put them into a barrel and lower them by a pulley that was fastened to the top of the building. I secured the end of the rope at ground level and went up to the top of the building, loaded the brick into the barrel, and flung the barrel out with the bricks on it. I then went down and untied the rope, holding it securely to insure the slow descent of the barrel.

As you will note in block No. 6 of the insurance form, I weigh 145 pounds. Due to my shock at being jerked off the ground so swiftly, I lost my presence of mind and forgot to let go of the rope. Between the second and the third floors I met the barrel, coming down. This accounts for the bruises and lacerations on my upper body.

Upon regaining my presence of mind, I held tightly to the rope and proceeded rapidly up the side of the building, not stopping until my right hand was jammed into the pulley. This accounts for my broken thumb.

Despite the pain, I retained my presence of mind and held tightly to the rope. At approximately the same time, however, the barrel of bricks hit the ground and the bottom fell out of the barrel. Devoid of the weight of the bricks, the barrel now weighed about 50 pounds. I again refer you to block No. 6 and my weight.

As you would guess, I began a rapid descent. In the vicinity of the second floor, I met the empty barrel coming up. This explains the injuries to my legs and lower body. Slowed only slightly, I continued my descent, landing on the pile of bricks. Fortunately, my back was only sprained and the internal injuries were minimal. I am sorry to report, however, that at this point I again lost my presence of mind and let go of the rope. As you can imagine, the empty barrel crashed down on top of me.

I trust that this answers your concern. Please know that I am finished "trying to do the job alone."
Yours sincerely.

The bricklayer discovered the hard way what church leaders are learning: trying to do the job alone can be a hazardous enterprise.

Why Build Ministry Action Teams?

A number of definitions have been offered for the concept of team ministry. Chuck Bowman often says, "A team is two or more people with two things in common: a shared goal and good communication." Jon Katzenbach and Douglas Smith provide more detail when they write, "A team is a small number of people with complementary skills who are committed to a common purpose, performance goals, and approach for which they hold themselves mutually accountable." R. Daniel Reeves puts it this way, "Team ministry is ownership and self-initiated vision in which members carry out plans they themselves have conceived or have had a part in conceptualizing." Basically, team ministry refers to a group

The great strength of the church is that people don't work for a living—they work for a cause.

—Peter Drucker

of church leaders working together for the purpose of building God's kingdom. These Ministry Action Teams will be vital to the success of the church in this new century.

The key to understanding the value of Ministry Action Teams is found in the word "action." These teams exist *so that something might be accomplished*. Ministry Action Teams are characterized by three important traits:

1. Shared vision and values. A powerful synergy is created when leaders work together for common objectives: *Behold, how good and how pleasant it is for brethren to dwell together in unity . . . for there the LORD commanded the blessing—life forevermore* (Ps. 133:1, 3). Every Ministry Action Team needs to fully understand the church's mandate: *Go therefore and make disciples of all the nations, baptizing them in the name of the Father and of the Son and of the Holy Spirit, teaching them to observe all things that I have commanded you; and lo, I am with you always, even to the end of the age* (Matt. 28:19-20). And every church must fully understand that this primary goal given by our Lord cannot be achieved without a unity of purpose and an anointed team effort. In other words, the church must get its act together!

2. Biblical models. Ministry is best performed in concert with other believers. The church must return to the biblical norm that so characterized the first-century church: *Continuing daily with one accord in the temple, and breaking bread from house to house, they ate their food with gladness and simplicity of heart, praising God and having favor with all the people. And the Lord added to the church daily those who were being saved* (Acts 2:46-47).

Driven by rapid church growth, the Jerusalem church, out of necessity, adopted a team approach to meet the rising demands.

Now in those days, when the number of the disciples was multiplying, there arose a murmuring against the Hebrews by the Hellenists, because their widows were neglected in the daily distribution. Then the twelve summoned the multitude of the disciples and said, "It is not desirable that we should leave the word of God and serve tables. Therefore, brethren, seek out from among you seven men of good reputation, full of the Holy Spirit and wisdom, whom we may appoint over this business; but we will give ourselves continually to prayer and to the ministry of the word."

And the saying pleased the whole multitude. And they chose Stephen, a man full of faith and the Holy Spirit, and Philip, Prochorus, Nicanor, Timon, Parmenas, and Nicolas, a proselyte from Antioch, whom they set before the apostles; and when they had prayed, they laid hands on them. Then the word of God spread, and the number of the disciples multiplied greatly in Jerusalem, and a great many of the priests were obedient to the faith. And Stephen, full of faith and power, did great wonders and signs among the people *(Acts 6:1-8)*.

Obviously, a "team ministry" approach enabled the Jerusalem church to be much more effective than it otherwise would have been. May we have this similar outcome in our churches today: *The word of God spread, and the number of the disciples multiplied greatly.*

3. *Increased productivity.* More can be accomplished together than separately: *Two are better than one, because they have a good reward for their labor* (Eccles. 4:9). Two great Old Testament characters, Moses and Aaron, exemplify this principle. As you know, Moses was gifted in leadership but wasn't a communicator. What Moses lacked in communication, however, Aaron excelled in. As a team, they led God's people on a march to the Promised Land. Two were better than one!

It's the same in the church. *Dedicated* leadership should *delegate* tasks based on individual gifts with *determination* to fulfill a common goal. There are six specific ways that ministry effectiveness is increased by the development of Ministry Action Teams:

- They expand the power of information and ideas through networks of sharing.
- They establish community, thus meeting people's psychological and spiritual need to be with others.
- They enlarge ministry opportunities through specialization by focusing on spiritual gifts.
- They make it possible for improved learning and decision making to take place.
- They create synergy, which builds on the expanded possibilities and potentials of interfacing spiritual gifts and ministries.
- They help the church overcome the latent or residual effect of individual biases.

Not Just New Programs and Committees

Changing to a "team-building ministry" should not be approached like an afternoon jog. It is not just another exercise routine or "program" added to the existing list of things to do. Before attempting this change we should first build *focus, commitment,* and *spiritual grounding.*

The central issue in the move to a team ministry is to decentralize leadership. Although traditional committees involve "people doing ministry together," they have often been formed by simply recruiting from some other committee, and they often lack effectiveness.

A recent Focus on the Family survey of pastors in 36 different denominations revealed that unrealistic expectations from church committees were a major source of frustration. Could it be that most of the burnout and restlessness among pastors comes from spending long hours with committees that show only marginal progress? Again, Roberta Hestenes says, "We must ruthlessly control the number and quality of the meetings in our lives if we are to avoid the 'numb pastor syndrome.' If our meetings can be transformed into the effective work of teams, we will see God renew, build, and use our people in a more helpful and effective way."

A special committee of dignitaries was appointed to meet the missionary statesman Dr. Albert L. Schweitzer on his visit to America in the '50s. Upon his arrival, the distinguished committee members lining the platform of the train station noticed that the doctor seemed to be looking past them toward the crowd. Much to the dismay of the welcoming committee, someone else had caught his eye.

With a cursory handshake, Schweitzer excused himself and went to an elderly woman in the crowd who was struggling with a large suitcase. Picking up the woman's luggage, he led her through the crowd, past the welcoming committee, to the steps of the train's passenger car. Dr. Schweitzer helped her up the steps, into the train car, and put her heavy suitcase in the overhead rack. Afterward, he went back to the distinguished committee and apologized for their wait. The welcoming committee had a "concern," but Dr. Schweitzer had a "cause."

Unfortunately, many church committees have a "concern" rather than a true biblical "cause." Very little time is given to advancing the Kingdom by vision casting, strategic planning, or evangelism and discipleship. In fact, as a church gets larger, it becomes increasingly more difficult to become proactive in these vital areas of ministry. Why? The pastor and other paid staff often get caught up in merely facilitating traditional programs.

Furthermore, churches under the "committee" system usually grow only to the energy level of the senior pastor. When the pastor runs out of steam, the church loses any momentum that has been built up, and this often results in discouragement and low morale in the church. **Ministry Action Teams, however, are much more effective.**

In his book *Team Building: An Exercise in Leadership,* Robert B. Maddux makes a distinction between *groups* and *teams.* While *teams* are characterized by members who recognize their interdependence and common goals, *groups* are often merely a number of people working independently, though side by side. While members of a *team* feel a sense of ownership, members of a *group* see themselves more as "hired hands," since they are not involved in planning the group's objectives.

Maddux further cites a study of 20 coal mines. The study illustrates the increased productivity that results from going beyond the "group" paradigm to actual "teamwork." The coal mines were in the same geologic structure, drew from the same labor pool, and were subject to the same governmental regulations. Productivity was measured in tons of coal produced per employee, per shift. The mine with the highest productivity delivered 242 tons per employee, contrasted with the lowest, which mined 58 tons per employee.

The study concluded that the primary difference in the mines was the way in which company management worked with the employees. The most productive mines provided employees with significantly more individual responsibility and involvement in goal setting and problem solving.

While the establishment of ministry teams may be difficult, the final joys far outweigh the "growing pains."

• Increased lay involvement

- A willingness to do things differently
- Team ownership instead of individual ownership
- An exciting climate in which to minister
- Unity and enthusiasm
- Clear ministry focus
- Encouragement as the norm

The natural world gives several examples of shared leadership. Engineers have used wind tunnels to calibrate why flocks of geese always fly in the V formation. They discovered that each goose, when flapping its wings, creates lift for the bird flying next to it in formation. The entire flock gains more than 70 percent greater flying range than one goose flying alone. From time to time, the lead goose falls back from the point position and another assumes the lead without breaking the formation. Every goose takes the lead during a long migratory flight. Each contributes his or her unique talents to the overall effectiveness of the flock. It should also be noted that the geese who are following honk to encourage the one leading.

Eph. 4 and the Corporate World

There is a crisis in most local churches today. Pastoral staff and laypersons put in long hours but see few lasting results. In Eph. 4:11-13 the apostle Paul describes the primary function of leaders. According to verse 12, they equip the *saints for the work of ministry, for the edifying of the body of Christ, till we all come to the unity of the faith and of the knowledge of the Son of God, to a perfect man, to the measure of the stature of the fullness of Christ.*

Pastors of growing churches have already discovered that the job of pastoral ministry is simply too big for one person to handle alone. As Ronald E. Merrill and Henry D. Sedgwick have pointed out, "[Churches] beyond a certain size [about 150] cannot be managed by a single person; a management team is required" (*INC* magazine, August 1994). Although most pastors haven't been taught much

> *No matter how much work you can do, no matter how engaging your personality may be, you will not advance far in business if you cannot work through others.*
>
> —John Craig

about ministry teams in Bible college and seminary, learning how to form successful teams is crucial to the long-term health of a growing church.

The corporate world models some of the best ways those teams should function. Many corporate leaders have already discovered the usefulness of teamwork, not realizing that it is a principle established in the pages of Scripture thousands of years ago. However, church leaders must be quick to recognize the critical difference between corporate marketplace teams and ministry teams in the local church. According to Reeves,

The core beliefs of church leaders form the foundation for team ministry: Our convictions about humility and brokenness come from God, not popular psychology. Prayer and the study of God's Word, not management theory books, create the passion for team ministry and prompt our desires to yield to God's will. It is God who is the instigator and sustainer of healthy, functional team relationships. (R. Daniel Reeves, *Ministry Advantage* 8, No. 1)

Team Styles

While the Bible must always be our foundation for the team model, the corporate world can teach us some practical lessons on how leadership teams function.

Notice three different team styles from the corporate business world.

Employee teams. In businesses that have employee teams, there still is a key decision maker that sets the policies and goals. This person has the ultimate control and the team literally works *for* him or her. Two important questions are raised in trying to use such a model in a church setting: (1) Do you, as the senior pastor, really want that much control? And, (2) Is this the kind of leadership and discipleship philosophy you want to foster? The corporate world and the church share one thing: **The key to effective employee teams is giving each team member a sense of significance.**

Small partnerships. In this corporate model, the leader exchanges some of his or her control for shared ownership. The leader is then able to enjoy the assistance of team members who have a real stake in the success of the organization. In comparison with the members of an "employee team," colleagues in this type of organization are generally more highly motivated.

Big-team ventures. In major corporations, teams with lots of talented individuals have the potential to accomplish great things—if the individuals can function well as a team. High-powered management teams in the corporate world require a self-confident leader and a sense of shared equity among the team members.

Stopping Failure Before It Starts

Larry Gilbert owned an electric sign business. He learned much about leadership by managing his company through the ups and downs of business. Because of the type of business, all his customers were businesspeople. Over the years, he observed these businesses and saw many of them come and go.

In fact, he watched 90 percent of these new businesses fail within their first five years. The reason they failed was usually a result of their owners' inability to lead and manage. These businesspeople failed to manage the resources available to them. They failed to manage their time and money and, most importantly, they failed to lead and manage the people they had gathered to help them carry out their dreams and goals.

On the other side of the spectrum, most *successful* businesses never fulfill the dreams their owner and founders envisioned. Again, the lack of ability to lead and manage puts uncontrolled limitations on these businesspeople. Through Gilbert's years of self-employment and the opportunity to work with, and evaluate, literally hundreds of businesses, he determined that success in business can be reduced to one simple leadership principle: **The size of every business is regulated by the leadership capacity of its owner.**

After being called into the ministry and working in churches, Gilbert, like many Christian leaders, ignored the principles he had learned from secular business. His logic was that anything secular could not apply to the church. However, he quickly realized that since these principles are biblical, they are just as valid in the church as they are in any business. In fact, he soon revised his success principle to read: **The size of every church is regulated by the leadership capacity of its pastor.** He began to formulate a distinct parallel between leadership in business and leadership in the church.

Leadership is not something that starts at the low end of the spectrum and grows at a steady incline until it reaches its maximum. Leadership is developed on plateaus. For businesspeople (or pastors) to expand their capacity in leadership, they must grow within these plateaus.

Plateaus of Leadership

Plateau No. 1. In business the first plateau of leadership is the *owner/operator*. This individual goes into business for himself or herself and does everything that needs to be done. He or she owns it and operates it—makes the product, does all the office functions, sweeps the floors, scrubs the toilets, does whatever needs to be done. The owner/operator is usually an entrepreneur—a person who is willing to go out on the limb and take all the risks.

In the church, the first plateau may be called the *church planter*. The church planter starts a church, or simply takes over a smaller church, and does basically the same thing as the owner/operator in business. This person takes care of the "business" of the church—prepares and preaches the sermons, serves as the Sunday School superintendent, and teaches Sunday School. Basically, just like the business owner/operator, the church planter does *everything* that has to be done in the church. And at this stage of the game, this might be OK. The church planter may be the only one qualified to do the job, and the job must be done. However, this single-handed role just shouldn't continue forever.

Plateau No. 2. Plateau No. 2 has the same effect for the businessperson as for the pastor-leader. They both realize they can no longer do it *all* themselves. How do they know? It's simple: Their spouses are threatening to leave them! Their time is *consumed* with their business or their church. They no longer have time for family or any other activities. They find that they cannot work 28 hours per day, and they soon come to the conclusion that if their business (or ministry) is going to prosper, they will need a team. **They must delegate some of these tasks to others.**

However, instead of fully stepping up to Plateau No. 2 and becoming *managers,* many businesspeople mistakenly fall into what is called the "founder's trap" and become *proprietors.* (The term "proprietor" is typically associated with *smaller* businesses.) Proprietors decide to hire people to help them. The proprietor falls into the founder's trap because he or she has not learned how to build a *team.* When the proprietor hires helpers, that is all they are—helpers. The boss still drives the truck; the helper goes along to hand the tools.

The boss still does the paperwork; the helper "assists" with clerical functions. What the proprietor fails to do is to utilize the strengths of the helper. The helper is only given some distasteful duties such as cleaning the toilet, stocking the shelves, or simply "helping" with the tasks.

If the businessperson does not learn how to develop a team and remains instead in the same relationship with the one, two, or three helpers, the business's growth is hindered because growth still directly revolves around the function of the owner. In essence, the owner has become the limiting factor to the size of the business.

In church ministry, pastors also fall into the founder's trap and become what we call *Ephesians 4 servants*. Instead of becoming *leaders* of their people, their role is limited to being *servants* to their people. Again, everything revolves around the pastors, and they become the limiting factor to the size of their church.

For the businessperson that does not get caught in the founder's trap, the next step or plateau should be to become a *manager*. Managers hire a team to work *for* them. They equip and lead their team to carry out the "purpose" of the organization.

In the church, the next plateau for the pastor is to become an *Ephesians 4 pastor* who leads, feeds, and equips the people. In Eph. 4:11-12, certain gifts are mentioned, including "pastor-teacher": *And He Himself gave some to be apostles, some prophets, some evangelists, and some pastors and teachers, for the equipping of the saints for the work of ministry, for the edifying of the body of Christ.* The pastor was given for the *equipping of the saints for the work of the ministry.* That means the pastor is "coaching" the saints—building team members for the work of the ministry—so that the Body of Christ may be edified. In other words, the pastor (coach) equips the "team" so *they* can do the work of the ministry.

Instead of hiring staff like the businessperson, the Ephesians 4 pastor takes advantage of the workforce already available—the laypeople—a team of Christians already gifted by God. The pastor (coach) trains them to *utilize* their gifts. This provides all the workforce needed. When the pastor can no longer lead the team alone, then, and *only then*, should additional staff be hired.

Ephesians 4 pastors are stewards of the gifts, talents, and abilities of those entrusted to their care. A true Ephesians 4 pastor says, "I am not here to do the work of the ministry by myself. I am here to equip my people, build them up, train them, and educate them so they will be enabled for ministry." The job of Ephesians 4 pastors is twofold: (1) To develop the spiritual gifts of their team and, (2) to provide areas of service where they can exercise those gifts.

As the church grows, more help will be needed. To avoid prematurely hiring staff, pastors should first draw help from their congregation. If they hire more staff before that, they are sending their church in the wrong direction and will train their staff to do the same thing they are doing—*the work of the ministry* rather than involving the laypeople. At best, they are building a "spectator" church.

Even when the pastor learns to train laypersons for ministry, the time may come when an Ephesians 4 pastor cannot alone train and keep all the laypeople involved. Such a pastor must eventually become a *multistaff pastor*, working with the laypeople and training them to minister first. Then, when paid staff is added, they will all be going in the same direction. The added staff will continue what the pastor started — training and leading the laity to do the work of the ministry.

Plateau No. 3. In business, the next plateau is the *executive stage*. Basically, the *executive's* job, like the manager's, is to manage people. The executive studies, analyzes, gives direction, and motivates, managing the team by *managing the managers*. The managers in turn manage the workforce.

On the church side, Plateau No. 3 involves the multistaff pastor who delegates responsibility to the staff team. The staff oversees the church team—the laity. When the pastor says, "Staff, here is what *we* need to do," he or she wants them to see that it gets done. Pastors should delegate through the laity *before* they delegate to a staff person, and they should train their staff to do the same. In that way, laypersons become an extension of the pastoral staff ministry.

Getting to the Next Plateau

Pastors must grow through one plateau to get to the next. They cannot successfully go from the church-planter stage straight to the multiple staff. Coaching is the only way to become a true Ephesians 4 pastor. Pastors "coach" in a team ministry, members learning what their gifts are and understanding where they fit into the ministry of the church. Pastor-coaches also understand that exercising their gift is part of a team effort with the rest of the Body of Christ, enabling a dynamic release of ministry both within the church and outward to a lost world.

To some, building these teams can seem to be an enormous and daunting task that works only for those pastors who are already "successful." That need not be the case. Team building can occur, and should occur, with any pastor, regardless of the location or size of the congregation. However, **the first step in building a "team" is for the pastor to begin to think of himself or herself as a "coach" who directs a group of special teams, not a servant who tries to meet *all* the needs of the congregation.** Even before the teams are created, the pastor must have a clear concept of what it means to function as a pastor-coach.

On *Leadership Today* Dale Galloway pointed out that teams made up of the laity could easily perform the majority of functions currently occupying the schedule of most pastors.

Dale said, "Ten ministry activities often fill a parish pastor's day." (See list below and check only those activities that laity could *not* share with the pastor.)

- Pray for the congregation
- Care for the sick
- Disciple other believers
- Train ministry leaders
- Study and teach the Bible
- Tell others about Jesus
- Represent the church at community events
- Visit newcomers to the church
- Run errands for the church office
- Encourage people through hard times

If pastors truly shared ministry based on the Spirit-anointed gifts of lay ministry teams, I don't think we would find anything that they could *not* do in ministry! Church history teaches that whenever clergy become the elite ministry "doers," the congregations they serve stagnate and die.

By A.D. 300, the church was growing so fast that, conceivably, the whole world could have been converted during the next 200 years. But the emperor, Constantine, made a near-fatal error. He decreed that everyone in the Roman Empire was already a "Christian." People who didn't really *know* Christ couldn't *introduce* Christ to others. An elite clergy and a pagan laity put the growth of Christianity on hold. Conversely, when lay believers in Christ joined with each other—and with the clergy—in meaningful team ministry, the church thrived.

Perhaps you should hang this helpful acronym on your

> The church of the future will enlarge the kingdom of Jesus Christ by a multiplication of care through shared ministry with lay pastoral caregivers.
>
> —Carl George

office wall as a reminder of the fruitfulness that comes with team ministry:

Together
Everyone
Achieves
More Ministry

Defining the Teamwork Vision

Team building is not something that will happen automatically. The pastor must have a clear vision for it. Consider these four goals for team ministry in the local church:

1. Organizing the team to discover and fulfill the Great Commission
2. Empowering the team to reach the community for Christ
3. Communicating ministry accomplishments to the congregation
4. Relating to one another in a manner that pleases God

Ready or not, we are on the verge of a major reformation in the very nature of how we have been "doing church." This reformation is absolutely necessary if the church is to minister effectively in the next century. Melvin Steinbron, after observing the changes in the lay ministry's role over four decades, concludes, "In the first reformation, the church gave the *Bible* to the people. In the second reformation, the church gave the *ministry* to the people." Elton Trueblood, a pioneering writer about the need for lay ministry, wrote in even stronger terms, "If the average church would suddenly take seriously the notion that every lay member—man or woman—is really a minister of Christ, we could have something like a revolution in a very short time."

Generation	Percentage Reached for Christ
Builders (Born before 1946)	65%
Boomers (Born between 1946 and 1964)	35%
Busters (Born between 1964 and 1977)	15%
Bridgers (Born between 1977 and 1994)	4%

Eighty-one percent of Christians accepted Christ before they were 20 years old, and the youngest busters and oldest bridgers are already over 20. This indicates that, without some drastic changes, we stand very little chance of reaching much of the two younger generations for Christ.

The subject of change was addressed in *The McIntosh Church Growth Network* newsletter (December 1998), "Minor changes are small modifications made without a corresponding shift in the perception of reality. Major changes occur when people develop a new perspective and act in new ways . . . Transformational change comes only through radical modification in belief and practice."

It's time for "transformational change." It's time for a new way of thinking about church ministry. It's time to train a host of "coaches" (Ephesians 4 pastors) who will call their team players (laypersons) from the *comfort zone* of the bench to the *courage zone* of the playing field and influence our world for Christ—while there is still time!

Team-Building Tips
- Share team mission, vision, and values at an annual retreat gathering.

- Ask ministry teammates what you can do to help them do a better job.
- Give positive reinforcement for skills enhanced and developed.
- Update team members frequently on ministry progress.
- Instead of "great idea, but not for us," try, "great idea— let's try it!"
- Remember the names and interests of your ministry team members.
- Give team members the resources they need to do the job.
- Provide a learning environment.
- Try reaching a consensus. A majority vote does not guarantee validity.
- Establish deadlines, then measure the team's ability to meet those deadlines.
- Let the team determine the deadlines.
- Cultivate a sense of ownership for the vision with the entire team.

2

Developing Coaching Skills

Who then is Paul, and who is Apollos, but ministers through whom you believed, as the Lord gave to each one? I planted, Apollos watered, but God gave the increase. So then neither he who plants is anything, nor he who waters, but God who gives the increase. Now he who plants and he who waters are one, and each one will receive his own reward according to his own labor. For we are God's fellow workers; you are God's field, you are God's building.

(1 Cor. 3:5-9)

WHILE COACHING FOOTBALL at the University of Colorado, Bill McCartney dared his 1991 team to play beyond their normal abilities. He had heard that most people spend 86 percent of their time thinking about themselves and only 14 percent of their time thinking about others. The coach was convinced that if his team could stop thinking about themselves and began to think of others, a whole new source of energy would be available to them.

McCartney challenged each player to call someone they loved and tell that person that they were dedicating the game to him or her. The team members were to encourage those persons to carefully watch every play they made, because the game was dedicated to them. McCartney arranged to distribute 60 footballs, one for each player to send to the person he had chosen, with the final score written on the football.

Colorado was playing its arch rival, the Nebraska Cornhuskers, on Nebraska's home turf. Colorado had not won a game there in 23 years, but Coach McCartney challenged

> *Coaching is eyeball-to-eyeball management.*
>
> —Dennis C. Kinlaw

his players to go beyond themselves—to play for love. The Colorado Buffaloes won the game, and the score written on 60 footballs was "27 to 12."

What Makes a Great Coach?

Why do some teams attain levels of achievement far beyond the individual talents of the team members? It always involves a great coach and committed team members. As Darrell Royal once said, "The coach is the team, and the team is the coach. You reflect each other."

Successful coaches aren't always recognized for their achievements. In fact, the most effective coaches may seem to be invisible at times. As Lao-Tsu once said, "When the best leader's work is done, the people say, 'We did it ourselves.'"

According to John Maxwell, "Your success as a spiritual coach is directly dependent on your ability to influence your leaders." In this context, Maxwell has designed the "3M Coaching Model," which stresses that an effective leader fills three roles:

1. *A model.* Most of us learn about 80 percent of what we know from what we observe. So the best way to convey the qualities needed for successful teamwork is to demonstrate them. If you want team members to be dedicated, then you must show them your commitment. If they are expected to put the team first, then the coach makes sacrifices too. If you want them to care for each other, then you must demonstrate your love for them. There's no substitute for showing them what you expect. Again, the apostle Paul wrote to his team, *For you yourselves know how you ought to follow us, for we were not disorderly among you; nor did we eat anyone's bread free of charge, but worked with labor and toil*

night and day, that we might not be a burden to any of you, not
because we do not have authority, but to make ourselves an ex-
ample of how you should follow us (2 Thess. 3:7-9).

2. A mentor. Good coaches also mentor their teams.
They add value to their people by helping them grow, by encouraging them to be their very best. Like the New Testament's Barnabas, they are quick to give a good word of affirmation. Coaches who mentor team members see them
not as they are but as they could be—building on the
strengths of their team, teaching them how to shore up
their weaknesses. Mentors are much more than advisers.
While advisers may stand passively by and give opinions,
mentors come alongside their people and walk with them
during the most difficult parts of their journey. Great pastor-
coaches not only watch from the sidelines but are actively
involved in the game.

3. A motivator. Coaches who want their teams to
succeed must motivate the players. Parkes Robinson says,
"Motivation is when your dreams put on work clothes." For
a group of people to come together as a team and to accomplish their goal, they need to move from "great potential" to "great performance." They need to "put on their
work clothes," and that requires motivation. Coaches must
inspire their players with vision, praise their contributions,
and give them incentives. People need to be shown how
their vision lines up with the team's. They need to understand that a win for the team is a win for them personally.

Most people respond to team leaders they trust. Successful ministry "coaching" is more than a matter of understanding the mechanics of leading people. It also requires an
ability to *relate* to people. President Abraham Lincoln had a
clear understanding of this principle when he said, "If you
would win a man to your cause, first convince him that you
are his sincere friend."

Also, ministry "coaching" is never complete without the element of *training*. Seldom will the members of our church teams come to us fully equipped and fully trained. We must give them the necessary tools and resources that will help them develop their God-given talents and abilities.

Great coaches have the following characteristics:

They have a high self-esteem. Coaches must have a confidence in their ability to lead the team. It seems that everyone struggles with the self-esteem issue. But those issues can be settled when we see ourselves as valuable because of Christ's love for us, not because of something we can (or cannot) do. Ministry coaches need to understand that God has a lofty opinion of them! The psalmist captured the essence of that in his Spirit-anointed words, *You have formed my inward parts; You have covered me in my mother's womb. I will praise You, for I am fearfully and wonderfully made; marvelous are Your works, And that my soul knows very well* (Ps. 139:13-14).

They are goal-driven. Coaches have a game plan, and they teach their teams to focus on the *plan* instead of the *problem*. You've probably seen professional coaches pace the sidelines with a piece of paper in their hands, referring to it before and after every play. That piece of paper has the game plan on it. It tells the coach what must be done if the team play is to result in victory. God has given us the game plan, *This Book of the Law shall not depart from your mouth, but you shall meditate in it day and night, that you may observe to do according to all that is written in it. For then you will make your way prosperous, and then you will have good success* (Josh. 1:8). Successful ministry coaches focus on God and His plan for their lives.

They are good communicators. Coaches may have great knowledge and experience in their sport, but to be effective, they must know how to communicate that knowledge and experience to their team. Jesus Christ (the Master Coach) never had trouble communicating with His team. They knew exactly what their ministry objectives were—beginning at Jerusalem, then on to the uttermost parts of the earth. Ministry coaches are well advised to study His communication skills. And those same coaches can turn to Him as a source of wisdom in communicating their heart to their congregation.

They are flexible. Coaches have to learn how to make on-the-spot changes. Circumstances arise, such as an injury to a vital member of the team, that call for coaches to put their confidence in another player to finish out the game. And sometimes even the game plans must be revised. Some circumstances call for "Plan B." Successful coaches know when it's time to call a new set of plays.

Ministry coaches must learn to do the same thing. The "We've always done it this way" approach to ministry often leads to being "thrown for a loss." There are times when a new play—and even a new player—may result in a significant "gain." Pastor-coaches should be flexible enough to accept each believer as a significant member of God's team and to appreciate the uniqueness that He has given them.

They are relational. To be effective as a coach, coaches must relate well to their players. Some of time's greatest coaches have been their player's greatest friends. Golfing great Tiger Woods points to his relationship with his coach (who was also his dad) as one of the leading factors in his success. Tiger's father taught him not only the skills that have made him a champion but also about love and trust and loyalty.

Eph. 4 not only tells the ministry "coach" how to communicate ministry skills to the congregation but also tells him or her how to build relationships with the members of the congregation. *Be kind, tenderhearted, and forgiving* (v.

32). The pastor-coaches who incorporate these relational guidelines into their ministry find the congregation eager to respond in like manner.

They are supportive. Good coaches learn how to capitalize on their players' strengths, and how to show compassion toward their weaknesses. Coaches must know how to work with both the strength and the weakness of their team and support them accordingly.

The pastor-coach will always be supportive of his or her team, no matter their strengths or weaknesses. But first, that leader must learn to allow God to support him or her. It's too easy to get so wrapped up in the game and "serve God" without remembering that we must first learn to lean on Him. Only when we've learned to be a "leaner" can we truly be a "leader," empathizing with those who must lean on us.

They are passionate. Coaches are not afraid to show emotion. Some of the most well known coaches in sports have been those who have openly displayed their feelings— and some of those displays have been notorious.

Jesus Christ himself showed a wide range of passionate emotions—from love to anger and from sorrow to joy. Remember that the Christ who gathered little children to himself in fatherly love also drove the moneylenders from the Temple in righteous indignation. Our culture often conditions us to hide our passion, but leaders who express a passion for their mission with a Christlike sincerity and a Spirit-controlled temperament motivate congregations.

They are motivated. Coaches don't depend on their teams to motivate them. They are already motivated, and their teams become motivated as a result.

Pray that God will ignite the fires of motivation in your heart. Pray that God will give you a burden to awaken the sleeping through vibrant team ministries. When your congregation feels and sees that motivation, the Holy Spirit will use it to motivate them.

They are patient. Professional coaches have higher expectations of a seasoned pro than a starting rookie. They know that part of their job is to be patient with the beginners until they develop into seasoned players.

When starting any new venture, it's easy to get discouraged if our high expectations aren't immediately met. High expectations are great, but a good dose of God-given patience will season our expectations and give us a balance that will help us fight discouragement.

They are forgiving. Good coaches don't focus on the mistakes of their players; they focus on the player's correct attitudes and actions. Good coaches learn to move on. Last week's bad game could be a forerunner of next week's good game! Every one of us needs to learn how to "move on."

Let God's forgiveness be a model for our forgiveness when dealing with church members who don't see our new vision and attempt to create dissension. Before you implement the "coach" paradigm, it would be wise to adopt an attitude of forgiveness for those who will inevitably get under your skin. Do what Christ did on the Cross and choose to "preforgive" any future troublemakers.

Five Coaching "Musts"

In addition, remember these five "musts" for becoming an effective coach to your team players from Alabama's legendary football coach Bear Bryant:

1. *Tell them what you expect of them.* Ministry team members should know how they fit into the game plan, and they should also know what you expect them to do to carry out that plan.

High performance expectations are consistently the best predictors of team success.

—Clay Carr

2. *Give them an opportunity to perform.* Team members should be given a chance to be a part of the "big picture" and carry out the vision.

3. *Let them know how they're getting along.* Verbal and written feedback gives team members an opportunity to learn, improve, and increase their contribution.

4. *Instruct and empower them when they need it.* Never be afraid to mentor the team when they seem uncertain. Always release and empower them to do the work after the training session.

5. *Reward them according to their contribution.* One example: at Trinity Church of the Nazarene in Oklahoma City, a partner in ministry is honored each month with a logo watch and a Five-Star Church Excellence Award Certificate.

Keeping the Team Alive

When we hear of someone's death, we often assume that the cause of death was some unpreventable physical problem, such as a massive heart attack, stroke, or cancer. Actually, there are at least three additional reasons why people die: (1) They run out of friends, (2) they run out of money, or (3) they run out of purpose. Similar causes of "death" may be seen in the local church ministry. Let's examine those causes, and see how Ministry Action Teams can be a great way of restoring life.

Friends. As a pastor, I (Toler) have often seen people in the local church give up on life when a spouse or a dear friend passes. They experience a mourning of the spirit that erodes their physical health—and often results in death.

I've also seen churches "get sick" and "die" when people "pass on" to another church because they didn't feel like they were a vital part of the previous church. Church growth consultants tell us that people need to bond with others if they are to remain active in a local church. They say that a visitor must establish a first-name friendship with seven to eight people or he or she will not remain in that church. Ministry Action Teams give people an opportunity to connect. The small-group nature of ministry teams gives them an opportunity for friendship and fellowship. **Ministry teams are kept alive through formal training times and informal fellowship times.**

Money. Some people have physical conditions, such as diabetes, that demand expensive medical treatment. The disease itself may not be fatal, but when health-care funds and adequate treatment are not available, it becomes a deadly circumstance.

Likewise, vital ministries in the church can be dealt fatal blows by both a lack of funds and inadequate care. Local churches must be trained in the importance of supporting new ministries—with their prayers and encouragement, as well as with their dollars. And church leaders must be challenged to "go the distance" in allocating funds for those ministries.

Ministry Action Teams shouldn't be put on "life support." If they are to be effective, they must be adequately supported. The pastor-coach must seek to **keep the team alive by clearly teaching the congregation about their value to the church's outreach and by "going to bat" for them in allocating funds for their ministries.**

Purpose. Comedian George Burns had a cute saying, "I can't die, I'm booked till I'm 100!" On the day he died *USA Today* announced, "And with no more bookings, George Burns died." We've all heard of people who gave up on life because they seemingly had no reason to live. **One key to keeping ministry teams alive is to constantly remind them of their purpose. A clearly defined, updated, and published statement of purpose for ministry**

teams is a great aid in maintaining ministry-healthy teams.

The Church's Leading Cause of Death

In fact, whole churches can die for those same reasons. If churches don't focus on their *purpose*, or if *friendships* aren't maintained and membership dwindles, it will automatically result in a lack of *funds*. They are deadly "diseases" that, if not corrected, will lead to the church's demise. However, a lack of members and a lack of funds can normally be corrected if a church will grasp a clear purpose for its existence. There is nothing sadder than a church (or an individual Christian) that has run out of purpose. Perhaps that is why the average life span of a church is only 30 years; the church simply loses its reason for existence: Knowing Christ and winning others to Him.

"Huddle Time"

One of the reasons sports teams huddle is to maintain their focus. In fact, a huddle serves a very important purpose for ministry teams as well. In addition to providing a time of focus, a huddle also *gives the team an opportunity to listen, allows time and opportunity for personnel changes to be made, provides an opportunity for plays to be called, and allows the team to rest.* Another key element in keeping Ministry Action Teams alive is to make certain the team members have periodic "huddle times."

Part of being an exceptional coach is understanding the dynamic of a team—what motivates them. Great coaches (and great pastor-coaches) are visionaries—they see things differently than other people do. They are not bosses, commanders, or dictators.

> Coaching is carrying out functions of leading, mentoring, tutoring, and confronting.
> —Tom Peters

QUALITIES OF EXCEPTIONAL PASTOR-COACHES

They know Christ.
They accept others.
They are flexible.
They enjoy challenges.
They are self-aware.
They value giftedness in others.
They are courageous.
They are supportive of others.
They keep agreements.
They share information freely.
They are filled with the Holy Spirit.
They listen.
They facilitate others.
They understand group dynamics.
They understand process improvement.
They know how to manage meetings.
They know how to manage projects.
They give feedback.
They can let go of personal agendas.
They resolve conflicts.
They are good communicators.

They know what "winning" looks like. They see their people as teammates—people with unique talents and a common purpose, not just a collection of individuals. They learn what makes the team "tick." They learn how to motivate each individual. Exceptional pastor-coaches are continually developing their coaching skills.

A sense of partnership motivates ministry team members to work even harder.

—Toler/Gilbert

Years ago, in a small farming town, a grain mill was nestled beside a stream that flowed out of the hills. The most evident part of the mill was the wheel that caught the water from the stream. Inside the building, an axle ran from the wheel to the grinding stone that ground the grain delivered by the farmers. The source of power for the grindstone came from the water in the stream that flowed into the wheel's paddles and turned them, thereby turning the grindstone.

One morning the miller came to work after a bad storm. Several trees in the area had fallen and caused a lot of debris to be thrown around. When the miller checked his building before opening the mill, he found there was only a trickle of water flowing down the stream. Limbs and other debris from the storm had dammed the stream, stopping the flow of water. There wasn't enough power to turn the huge wheel. Something had to be done.

The miller went inside and tried to turn the grinding stone himself. No matter how much strength he exerted, he couldn't turn it. Soon he realized that the day's work couldn't be completed unless he got power back to the paddle wheel. Finally, he did the most obvious thing. He walked upstream and cleared away all the debris and limbs that had clogged the stream. Soon the wheel moved, and the farmers were loading the flour and meal as fast as he could turn it out.

Ministry wheels can come to a standstill too. Pastors can allow the "debris" of traditional ministry duties to clog their source of power. A study published in *Pastor's Family* (February-March 1997) revealed that the "pastor's average work week is 50 to 60 hours, and 80% of pastors feel that they are not adequately compensated financially." If we're not careful, pastoral ministry can easily turn from delight to duty by continuing in the same traditional vein year after year, never really seeing any church growth (or new converts) and feeling comfortable in maintaining the status quo. When all the while, God wants to clear away the accumulated debris and breathe His Holy Spirit into the church in a new and awesome way.

But in order for this to happen, some changes must be made. We must allow God to remove the debris from our hearts, piece by piece, in order to get a new sense of His power and a renewed vision of what "working at full potential" means to Him. Like the miller, we need to get rid of the debris that clogs the power source and causes us to produce only a fraction of what God has envisioned for us.

On Becoming a Pastor-Coach

Coaches are generally made, not born. In other words, there are few people who are "natural" coaches. The great "coaching" skills we've discussed thus far must be learned. Making the change from a "traditional pastor" role to a pastor-coach will not be easy; the learning process will, at times, seem painful. Pastors tend to get set in their traditional ministry patterns and often find new methods difficult, especially when their church members are leery of change. Nonetheless, change must happen if we are to evangelize our communities. Let the following suggestions fuel the fires of change from being an ordinary pastor to an extraordinary pastor-coach:

Change yourself first! Your *attitude, habits,* and *focus*—all must change so that they are in line with the "coaching" paradigm. In terms of *attitude,* you must think like a "facilitator" not a "doer." With regard to *habits,* you must change from doing ministry by yourself to inviting others to partner in ministry. Also, with regard to *focus,* the key will be to focus on training the team.

The *New York Times* reported a change in the advertising campaign of a well-known cereal company. In their first TV commercials, the actor portrayed a "set in his ways," lethargic, and low-key older man. When sales began to decline, they knew they needed a new image—and some new commercials.

In the next series of commercials, the spokesperson, a veteran actor, underwent a complete makeover. Instead of portraying him in placid scenes of walking the dog or swinging on a porch swing, the advertiser shows him to be active and aggressive—riding horses, digging postholes, and building a corral. The TV spots were aimed at the growing older population and were intended to present them as a "take charge" generation. The increase in sales was dramatic.

The change in emphasis began in the mind of the actor. He had to convey an entirely different attitude to make the commercials work. A new presentation to a new generation demanded a new focus. It's the same in ministry. Pastors who want to effect change in their congregations and reach their communities in a new and exciting way must, first of all, experience change themselves.

Explain to your church why you've changed. Your new "coaching" philosophy should not come as a surprise. For example, you could preach a Sunday night series of sermons that outline a scriptural basis for the "coaching" philosophy. The congregation must be taught that change is needed if your church is to steadily win souls.

Reaching a new generation demands some new methods. Things change, but the message must never change. There is still one Savior and one way to be saved. But the methods for teaching that message are subject to overhaul "to serve the present age," as Charles Wesley reminded us in song.

A word of caution: A teaspoon of sugar makes the medicine go down! New methods must be mingled with old-fashioned affirmation, love, and a commitment to the welfare of your people. Force-feeding new ministries does not result in healthy churches.

Share the "Acts 6" model. In this well-known passage, the disciples were so consumed with temporal duties they were forced to abandon the eternal.

> Now in those days, when the number of the disciples was multiplying, there arose a murmuring against the Hebrews by the Hellenists, because their widows were neglected in the daily distribution. Then the twelve summoned the multitude of the disciples and said, "It is not desirable that we should leave the word of God and serve tables. Therefore, brethren, seek out from among you seven men of good reputation, full of the Holy Spirit and wisdom, whom we may appoint over this business; but we will give ourselves continually to prayer and to the ministry of the word." And the saying pleased the whole multitude. And they chose Stephen, a man full of faith and the Holy Spirit, and Philip, Prochorus, Nicanor, Timon, Parmenas, and Nicolas, a proselyte from Antioch, whom they set before the apostles; and when they had prayed, they laid hands on them. Then the word of God spread, and the number of the disciples multiplied greatly in Jerusalem, and a great many of the priests were obedient to the faith *(Acts 6:1-7).*

When the disciples could no longer focus on their ministry because of the mundane duties they were trying to do alone, they made a ministry change. And you'll notice that they appointed team members!

When you share the Acts 6 study with your congregation, you may want to remind them of the McDonald's corporation motto: "We can accomplish more together than we can alone."

Define the mission. This means determining and articulating questions such as *Who are we? What are we? Where* *are we going?* As author Stephen Covey says, "The statement of mission draws the organization together."

Paul Lee Tan, in his *Encyclopedia of 15,000 Illustrations*, tells of an experiment by the Minnesota Safety Council in which two drivers traveled the same 1,000-mile route in similar vehicles but at different speeds. The "fast" driver passed 2,000 cars, braked 1,339 times, and covered the distance in 20 hours and 12 minutes. The "slow" driver flowed with traffic, passed 13 cars, and braked 652 times. It took the latter driver 20 hours and 43 minutes—just 31 minutes longer than the fast driver. The fast driver used 10 gallons more gas, and his pulse rate rose, probably because of the tension caused by the risks he had taken.

Without a clear mission, church leaders can be just like the "fast driver." They expend a lot of effort, cover the same territory, but end up with a breathless—and tense—congregation. Conversely, church leaders who guide their parishioners with deliberate "travel plans" (mission) arrive at their destination with a sense of unified purpose and fulfillment.

Become a vision caster. After much prayer, compile and communicate a yearly vision strategy for growth. Share your need of assistance from the congregation and the pastoral staff team.

J. Winston Pearce, in his book *Planning Your Preaching* (Nashville: Broadman Press, 1987), discusses the "chart that gives direction to your dreams." His goal-setting advice includes:

1. Establishing both short-range and long-range goals
2. Setting up tangible and intangible goals
3. Learning to recognize obstacles and then getting rid of them, by going around them or solving them
4. Using initiative, imagination, and ingenuity
5. Determining where you are now in relation to your goals and measuring your progress on a regular basis

6. Setting realistic and reasonable dates for reaching your goals

7. Picturing in your mind the rewards that will be yours when you reach your goals

It's a chart that could be used in setting ministry goals as well. Vision casting is integral to the health of the local church. Congregations are strengthened in knowing that their leader has a clear direction for their future.

Involve others in ministry. It's very easy to fall into the lone ranger mind-set. Some pastors see the church as their own and think that if a job is to be done right they must either do it themselves or closely supervise it. The truth is, a pastor's congregation existed long before he or she arrived and will most likely continue long after he or she leaves. No pastor can afford to start seeing himself or herself as the reason the congregation exists. The pastor-coach clearly sees that he or she is there *because* of the congregation, and that the means to strengthen that congregation is through the active participation of its laity.

Continually clarify the journey. What parent hasn't spent the better part of a vacation trip answering the childhood query, "Are we there yet?" The young passengers want to know if Dad or Mom has them on the right course. They're also saying, "How far have we come?" and "How long will it take us to get to our destination?" That "Q&A" time is important to their sense of well-being.

It's the same when working with church ministry teams. They are assured in knowing that their leader has them on the "right route." Team members must be given a clear communication of the "coach's" expectations and objectives. The very definition of "team" suggests clear goals and objectives to which all team members are committed.

Simplify, simplify, simplify. As Dr. Robert Kreitner says, "Simplify it so that an eight-year-old can understand."

Former Green Bay Packer coach Vince Lombardi understood this success principle well. Once Lombardi was one of the speakers at a convention of coaches, and several of the other speakers had just described their elaborate offensive and defensive schemes. When Lombardi was asked his strategy, he replied: "I only have two strategies. My offensive strategy is simple: When we have the ball, we aim to knock the other team down! My defensive strategy is similar: When the other team has the ball, we aim to knock *all* of them down!"

Everything from training materials to ministry assignments should be given in the simplest terms.

Changes in the Lives of Developing Coaches

As already stated, *becoming a pastor-coach is a process* —something that requires ongoing training, development, and change. Developing "coaching" skills will take some time—and a few struggles. There are five lessons that are particularly crucial for pastors to learn in the early stages of their "coaching" development.

Lesson One: Realize that there are no perfect pastors. I like the story of the preacher who went to a corner convenience store to buy a newspaper. He picked up the paper and took it to the counter where he discovered that he had forgotten to bring any money with him—not even the 50 cents needed for the paper. He explained to the clerk with embarrassment, "I'm afraid I don't have 50 cents with me. I guess the only thing I can do is invite you to my church and preach a 50-cent sermon to you. But I'm afraid I don't have any 50-cent sermons!" he continued.

The clerk replied with a smile, "Don't worry about it, Preacher. I'll come twice!"

We won't meet the perfect pastor until we get to heaven. The bottom line is that we are human, and humans make mistakes! At times we will feel like it would be better to forget the whole "change thing." But don't despair! Those feelings are simply a part of the growing process. Regardless of the mistakes we may make, there are still souls near our churches who don't know the Lord, and those souls need our ministry—imperfect as it may be at times. God uses people who are willing to risk new methods to reach them.

Lesson Two: Admit that a pastor's work is never done. Some folks in the secular world complete their assignments. Cases are closed. Land is contracted. Games are won. Buildings are built. The pastor's job is like the proverbial complaint, "A woman's work is never done." There is always something more to do. More lost souls to win, more marriages to save, more sermons to preach, more lessons to teach, more administrative duties to oversee, and more leaders to train.

Someone once said, "Great masterpieces are created by men out of breath." Our time on earth is short. We are following the One who said, *I must work the works of Him who sent Me while it is day; the night is coming when no one can work* (John 9:4).

Of course there will be long days. And of course we will want to sit down by the "well" as Jesus did. But we picked up the cross knowing that the journey would be difficult at times. Our work on earth is never done.

Lesson Three: Focus on your gifts. Everything goes better when we operate in our areas of giftedness instead of merely "reacting" to every area of need. Dr. Elmer Towns teaches a principle he calls "the division of labor," based on 1 Cor. 3:9, *For we are laborers together with God.* His principle simply states, "God will not do what He has commanded you to do, and you cannot do what God has reserved as His authority."

Lesson Four: Concentrate on your calling, not your critics. One study found that when a pastor is removed from a church, it is usually done by only about eight disgruntled people. The loudest voices around you may not be the voice of God for your ministry. There's a lot of power in being able to smile and say, "I'm sorry that you feel that way, but I love you and God loves you," and go on with the task the Lord has assigned to you. You do not have to defend yourself against every criticism, which you undoubtedly will receive. That only deflects energy from your calling and places your focus on the negative.

Remember, many of your critics see their own faults in you. Psychologists tell us that the things we don't like about others are the same things we have dormant in our own lives.

Lesson Five: Never stop learning. No matter how long you have been in ministry, it is vital that you maintain a teachable spirit and a willingness to change and grow. Henry Ford pointed this out in a perspective that we may apply to team ministry: "Coming together is a beginning, staying together is progress, and working together is success." Don't ever think you've "arrived"—keep learning and growing.

The apostle said it, *Not that I have already attained, or am already perfected; but I press on, that I may lay hold of that for which Christ Jesus has also laid hold of me* (Phil. 3:12).

Five Keys to Improved Coaching Skills

In his book *On Becoming a Leader,* Warren Bennis lists several important principles for those who want to develop their coaching skills:

1. **"Leaders start with great people."** You can't create greatness with mediocrity. Group leaders spend the appropriate time to find the right contributors to the group. They are often generalists instead of specialists.

A church should be built with *people* in mind instead of *programs.* There is nothing inherently wrong with programs; they are simply organized means to reach an objective.

However, many churches make the mistake of building super organizations and super programs first, and then later try to fit their people into them. *Start* with the people and their gifts (building the church by building them).

Someone has said, "Never use a great people to build a great church, but use a great church to build a great people." On the contrary, we *should* use a great people to build a great church and then use a great church to meet the needs of a great people. It is an unending and wonderful cycle: people ministering to people through the living organism called the church.

Even the secular world agrees with the philosophy of building *people* first. Today's leadership gurus emphasize this philosophy, saying,

> The key to make man effective is to start with the person, find out what his strengths are, and put him in a position where he can make full use of his strengths. Never start with the job and make the man fit into the job or the program. Start with the man and make the job or the program fit into his strengths. This will automatically minimize and render harmless his weaknesses. This is being people-centered in leadership *(Drucker 1966, 75)*.

2. "Leaders create space for creativity." The more creativity, the greater the ministry! Every great group needs someone who can organize the genius of others. They must be pragmatic dreamers and know how to create the environments for great projects to be successful.

Milton Bradley wanted to establish a career in the late 19th century creating board games. In just a short while, his games were found in countless living rooms in America. But his creativity wouldn't be stopped there. He had another idea. As a proponent of the kindergarten movement, Bradley saw the need for toys and teaching materials in the kindergartens.

Milton Bradley began to produce educational toys for kindergartens, though at that time kindergartens were quite rare. He only had a few customers to begin with, but within a generation, there were more than 3,000 kindergartens and Bradley was manufacturing supplies for all of them—from crayons to child-size furniture.

Leaders must allow room for the Milton Bradleys of their church to set goals, adjust those goals, and set their sights on greater endeavors.

3. ***"Leaders inspire mission by operating from a passion-rich spirit."*** The mission is always beyond them. It so focuses individuals beyond themselves that they make great sacrifices for the cause. People are recruited to crusades, not jobs.

Some folks are like the little girl who gave her version of the Lord's Prayer, "And lead us not into creation but deliver us from eagles." They are content to live in the land of "Status Quo," afraid to try new methods or soar to new heights. Leaders are just the opposite. They sing with the songwriter, "Still praying as I'm onward bound, 'Lord, plant my feet on higher ground.'"

What better cause is there to be passionate about than the church? It is the living, breathing body of a Risen Christ. It offers hope to the hopeless, healing to the hurting, and forgiveness to the guilty through its head, the Messiah!

4. ***"Leaders galvanize response, both to the mission and the 'competition.'"*** Leaders focus on defeating the real enemy. They stand against Satan's intent to "tangle the church in the cobwebs of antiquity," as someone once said. They caution the team to move from "We used to do it this way" to "Let's try another way." Pastor-coaches will offer a challenge to the church to bring down the strongholds of the Enemy (our real competitor) and build the kingdom of God in a refreshingly new, Spirit-led, positive, goal-oriented way. Paul Lee Tan wrote,

After Mary Magdalene left the tomb (John 20:17-18) there is no evidence that any believer ever returned to it. Furthermore, there is no Gospel evidence that any of the enemies of Jesus ever visited the tomb. His enemies did not go because they were *afraid* it was empty. Jesus' friends did not return to the tomb because they *knew* it was empty!

5. *"Leaders let the vision enable mission fulfillment in concrete ways."* Most church leaders are high on enthusiasm and low on planning. Churches need dreams with details and deadlines! Bennis was right when he observed, "Deadlines create the urgency to get the work done. They force creativity, not perfection."

President John F. Kennedy was once asked how he became a war hero. With his customary dry wit, Kennedy responded, "It was quite easy. Somebody sunk my boat!"

Many church leaders operate from a "sunken boat" strategy. Instead of careful (and prayerful) calendar planning, they create programs and utilize methods "just in time." Leaders could eliminate many administrative heartaches that come from last-minute plans and inadequate help by moving to a yearly calendar plan.

Add "Bench Strength" by Training Your Replacement

In his book *The Corporate Coach*, James B. Miller writes of the necessity for leaders to train their replacements—a process he calls "adding bench strength." He tells of one manager who learned this lesson the hard way:

> Several years ago a warehouse manager came to me with sugar plums dancing in his head. It was time for his annual review, and he couldn't wait to tell me about all the things he had accomplished in the past year. He was already counting the raise he was sure he was going to receive.

"I agree with you about your achievements. In fact, there are some additional things that you achieved that you don't have on your list," I said after he finished making his case. "You've set the world afire this year. I have one question for you, however. Who have you trained to take your place?"

"I don't have anyone."

"Neither do I!"

I then reminded him of the previous evaluations I had given him, how we both agreed that he would develop a successor so that he would be more promotable in the future as the company grew, and that there wouldn't be any additional pay increases until he had trained a replacement.

"Because you still don't have anyone in mind to take your place, I'm afraid we're going to have to hold off on any increase until you've trained a replacement."

He was shocked. But he began to take me seriously about the need to build bench strength. In fact, the next year, he had *two* people trained to replace him! All three of these individuals are still with us, and all have had promotions over the years because they developed replacements *(Miller 1993, 126-27)*.

Like the warehouse manager, many pastors initially resist the concept of training their replacements. After all, who wants to be replaced! Successful pastor-coaches, however, must focus on "adding bench strength." An excellent coach so instills purpose and so trains the team that they can literally win without him or her. Likewise, a good pastor-coach should leave in his or her wake a legacy of "fully trained" laypersons who know how to function as a team in the Body of Christ.

A splendid example of a pastor who did this so well is John C. Maxwell. When John resigned to direct his *Injoy* group full-time, he passed the Skyline Wesleyan ministry torch to Jim Garlow. With more than 1,600 trained leaders, Garlow has continued the tremendous growth pattern that Maxwell established in the Skyline Church.

On-site surveys at Injoy Model Church workshops have confirmed that the present pastoral philosophies in most churches include the following 10 expectations. As you carefully read this list, check which is a "pastor task" and which could be performed by a layperson:

1. Pastoral care
2. Administration
3. Performing rituals
4. Leading meetings
5. Preaching
6. Teaching
7. Counseling
8. Vision casting
9. Training staff
10. Recruitment

In addition, some churches expect their pastors to mow the church lawn and serve as the church custodian! With the exception of "Expectations" No. 5 and No. 8, all of the above tasks could be performed—and performed well—by laypersons, especially when they have been properly "coached."

To avoid confusion, pastor-coaches must clearly define the roles that are to be filled by their team members. Many Christians are aware of the tools (gifts) God has given them, but they don't know what they're to be used for: "Should I dig a hole with it—or saw a board, or use it to mix cement?" How can we expect laypersons to properly do the work of the ministry if they don't recognize which gifts they have and how they should use them? By showing them the purpose of the tools God has gifted them with and the way the tools work, we can strengthen the ministry of the team.

Team-Building Tips

- Clarify your team ministry goals monthly.
- Conduct a brainstorming meeting every six months.
- Teach team members the value of constructive criticism.
- State the purpose of all team meetings.
- Have a team photo gallery.
- Clearly define job duties, responsibilities, and priorities.
- Start all team meetings on time.
- Visit team members on their turf in order to save time.
- Create a day for sharing innovative team contributions.
- Give credit where credit is due.
- Monitor team performance.
- Share ministry successes with celebrations.

3

Using Biblical Guidelines for Effective Team Building

*Stand fast in one spirit, with
one mind striving together for
the faith of the gospel.*
(Phil. 1:27)

A STRANGER WALKING DOWN a residential street noticed a
man struggling to get a washing machine through the door-
way of his house. When the stranger volun-
teered to help, the homeowner was over-
joyed, and together the two men began to
struggle with the bulky appliance. After
several minutes of fruitless effort, the frustrated stranger said to the homeowner,
"We'll never get this washing machine in
there." The astonished homeowner replied,
"*In?* I'm trying to move it *out!*"

> The trouble with
> a mule is he is
> backward about
> going forward.
> —John R. Church

Effective teams communicate their
common goals and pull together in the
same direction. Paul told the Philippians to *stand fast in one
spirit.* Sadly, the church has evidenced a considerable
amount of pulling in *opposite* directions since that message
was first given.

The Four Cs of Successful Teamwork

Teamwork doesn't just happen. It is planned. It is
worked for. It is decided upon. Amateur or professional
sports may recruit teams. They may spend thousands (and
millions) of dollars for salaries, equipment, facilities, and

coaches. But dollars can't buy teamwork. It takes the individual effort of the coaching staff and the players. It's the
same in the church. Dollars can't buy teamwork. It comes
from the dedicated efforts of the "coach" and the ministry
team who possess some of the qualities found in these Four
Cs of teamwork:

Character. Team leaders must be believable and trustworthy. Ministry team members will not follow a person
who lacks integrity.

Dwight D. Eisenhower once said,

> In order to be a leader, a man must have followers.
> And to have followers, a man must have their confi-
> dence. Hence the supreme quality for a leader is un-
> questionable integrity. Without it, no real success is
> possible, no matter whether it is on a football field, in
> an army, or in an office. If a man's associates find him
> guilty of phoniness, if they find that he lacks forthright
> integrity, he will fail. His teachings and actions must
> square with each other. The first great need, therefore,
> is integrity and high purpose.

The wisdom writer gives us a Spirit-anointed vision of
the influence of godly character, *The righteous man walks in
his integrity; his children are blessed after him* (Prov. 20:7).

Cooperation. The apostle Paul encouraged the church
to *keep the unity of the Spirit in the bond of peace* (Eph. 4:3).
I'm appalled at the apparent bad behavior of some church
lay leaders. God calls the team to cooperation not division!

Every effort (and it will take effort) should be made to
avoid divisions and keep a spirit of unity. Cooperation is key
to successful ministries.

Communication. Team leaders must concentrate on
building an atmosphere that is conducive to good communication.

The axiom, "Say what you mean, and mean what you

say," certainly applies to the lines of communication that must be established between team leaders and their teammates.

Pat Summit, coach of the University of Tennessee Lady Volunteers, gave some excellent communication advice in a Bottom Line Personal interview:

1. Each person you are trying to motivate needs a different approach.
2. When giving positive reinforcement, emphasize the first and last things you say.
3. Talking is only one part of communication. Body language, facial expression, and—first and foremost—good eye contact are at least as important as the verbal message.
4. Be inspiring when you must be tough.

The apostle Paul taught about clear communication in his letter to the Corinthian Christians, *For if the trumpet makes an uncertain sound, who will prepare himself for battle? So likewise you, unless you utter by the tongue words easy to understand, how will it be known what is spoken? For you will be speaking into the air* (1 Cor. 14:8-9).

Commitment. A "Great Commitment to the Great Commission" is needed in every church team. Jesus reminded His disciples that following Him was an *all or nothing* proposition, *Then He said to them all, "If anyone desires to come after Me, let him deny himself, and take up his cross daily, and follow Me"* (Luke 9:23).

Andrew Carnegie once said, "The average person puts only 25 percent of his energy and ability into his work. The world takes off its hat to those who put in more than 50 percent of their capacity, and stands on its head for those few and far between souls who devote 100 percent."

The Apostle Models Team Building

Charles Haddon Spurgeon once said, "A man who has his Bible at his fingers' ends, and in his heart's core, is a champion in any conflict; you cannot compete with him; you may have an armory of weapons, but his Scriptural knowledge will overcome you."

With a Bible in their hands, pastor-coaches have the greatest resource for working with laypersons and building them into teams for ministry. From the organization of Moses to the training of the Master to the pastoral skills of the apostles, the Word of God is the administrative "lamp unto our feet" and "light unto our path."

In Rom. 15, the apostle Paul provides six keys to effective teamwork:

First, focus on God's Word. *That I might be a minister of Jesus Christ to the Gentiles, ministering the gospel of God* (v. 16). Paul was primarily a preacher and teacher of the gospel of Christ. Presenting the Word of God was a priority in his ministry—above all other duties. He also insisted that church leaders be students of God's Word. *Be diligent to present yourself approved to God, a worker who does not need to be ashamed, rightly dividing the word of truth* (2 Tim. 2:15).

His example establishes priorities for ministry teams in the local church. Though they may function in various ministry settings, their "main task" is to preach and teach the principles of God's Word. It may be taught by example, as in the case of a ministry team visiting the shut-in or serving a meal to the homeless. Or it may be taught by proclamation, as in the case of the Christian education team. But in every way, the Word of God must be foremost.

Second, seek to honor God in service. *Therefore I have reason to glory in Christ Jesus in the things which pertain to God* (Rom. 15:17). Too many chairpersons on today's church committees want the limelight. It's Christ's church and we must acknowledge His leadership over it. We are simply His servants.

We are followers of One who worked in a carpenter's shop and toweled the feet of His disciples. Our glory is not in certificates or honors banquets; it's in being faithful to the Master. Pastor-coaches and ministry teams are servants of the Lord.

Third, minister in the power of the Holy Spirit. *In mighty signs and wonders, by the power of the Spirit of God . . . I have fully preached the gospel of Christ* (v. 19). Church leaders must understand that organizational structures are simply a means to an end. They harness the power of others; they have no innate power. The power for successful church ministry comes from individuals who have been empowered by God.

The Old Testament writer reflected on that source in this prayer, *O LORD God of our fathers, are You not God in heaven, and do You not rule over all the kingdoms of the nations, and in Your hand is there not power and might, so that no one is able to withstand You?* (2 Chron. 20:6).

Pastor-coaches must instruct team leaders concerning the ultimate empowerment for all ministry. The Holy Spirit still works through those who will submit themselves to His cleansing and empowering.

Fourth, obey God. *I have made it my aim to preach the gospel, not where Christ was named, lest I should build on another man's foundation, but as it is written: "To whom He was not announced, they shall see; and those who have not heard shall understand"* (Rom. 15:20-21). Our Heavenly Father is not willing that any should perish. And His will is our will. Every team meeting should be opened with the prayer that says, "Thy will be done on earth as it is in heaven!"

Ultimately, what God is concerned about is what should concern the church. Our committees can make their plans to build sanctuaries but only as those sanctuaries are a place where the gospel is presented and where souls are given the opportunity to turn to the Savior!

Fifth, teach stewardship. *Now I am going to Jerusalem to minister to the saints. For it pleased those from Macedonia and Achaia to make a certain contribution for the poor among the saints who are in Jerusalem. It pleased them indeed, and they are their debtors. For if the Gentiles have been partakers of their spiritual things, their duty is also to minister to them in material things* (vv. 25-27). Team leaders and teammates truly worship God through their giving. Paul unashamedly asked his "partners in the gospel" to give unselfishly to the cause of Christ.

I like the story of the two church members who were talking about questions they would like to ask God. One said, "I'd like to ask Him why He allows poverty, famine, and injustice, when He could do something about it."

His friend said, "Well, why don't you go ahead and ask Him?"

"Because I'm afraid He'll ask me the same question!" the man answered.

Ministry team members must understand that God has placed resources in their hands that can be used to meet the material and spiritual needs of the world—starting in their own communities.

Sixth, enlist prayer partners. *Strive together with me in prayers to God for me, that I may be delivered from those in Judea who do not believe, and that my service for Jerusalem may be acceptable to the saints* (vv. 30-31).

In almost every case, when people were sent out in the Early Church, they were sent from a prayer meeting. It must be the same today. God works through the prayers of His people. *And when they had* prayed, *the place . . . was shaken* (Acts 4:31, emphasis added).

The highlight of every Sunday for me (Toler) is when my Trinity prayer partners gather around me and pray with me before I preach. There have been times when I felt so weak and ill prepared, and invariably in those moments the prayer team touched heaven for me.

There are people in our congregations who can't serve on a visitation team, work crew, building committee, or Christian education staff, but they can be intercessory prayer partners. They can bring heaven to earth to accomplish God's purpose through His people.

Teamwork and Team-Based Ministry

Successful churches will have a fruitful ministry not only to believers but also to the lost. In Rom. 15:14-22, Paul describes his ministry to the unconverted, while in verses 23-33 he deals with his ministry to Christians. For a church to have maximum impact, it must have ministry teams that address both areas.

In his book *Team Spirituality,* William J. Carter links the concept of teamwork and team-based ministry to the primary role of the church, which he divides into two subpoints: "The primary role of the church is to ensure that (1) persons find resources for their spiritual needs (grow closer to Christ, the head), and (2) employ themselves in expressing that spirituality in ways that demonstrate the presence of God in the body and in the world."

In defining the developmental stages or strategies of team building, Carter goes on to state:

We are not discussing here the formation of a group headed by a coach or manager dedicated to winning at any cost, or an arrangement that gives every person an assigned task that will result in a choreographed "play." In the church setting, the team is a group of persons with a defined spiritual objective developing an operations style and process that will enable them to achieve fruition . . . Team building is a series of activities that enables the team to discover its best operational style and maintain its process in order to fulfill its purpose and accomplish its objectives *(Carter 1997, 66).*

The Parable of Stacy King

Several years ago, *Newsweek* magazine interviewed Stacy King (a former Oklahoma Sooner basketball star) on a special night in the history of the Chicago Bulls basketball team. King commented, "It is a night I will always remember as the night that Michael Jordan and I combined to make 70 points." What Stacy King did not mention is that Michael Jordan scored 69 of those points—King scored only one! Yet, as Stacy King thought back on that night, he remembered that he actually assisted in the points Jordan scored. He remembered what they had done *together.*

The church should learn from the parable of Stacy King. You don't have to be a superstar in order to make a contribution. Stacy King couldn't jump as high or hang in the air as long as Michael Jordan. He never led the league in scoring or won a Most Valuable Player award. However, he was a productive member of the team.

Paul cited this same principle in his discussion with the Corinthians about spiritual gifts: *The eye cannot say to the hand, "I have no need of you"; nor again the head to the feet, "I have no need of you." No, much rather, those members of the body which seem to be weaker are necessary. And those members of the body which we*

> Successful leaders communicate to every ministry team member, "We need you! You are significant!"
> —Dave Sutherland

think to be less honorable, on these we bestow greater honor; and our unpresentable parts have greater modesty, but our presentable parts have no need (1 Cor. 12:21-24).

Stacy King's contribution to the Chicago Bulls was not the same as Michael Jordan's, but it was important nonetheless. Paul showed a profound understanding of teamwork when he said, *Those members of the body which seem to be weaker are necessary.*

The Necessity of Team Bonding

Paul's description of the church as being similar to a human body shows the importance of proper bonding. He says the members need to be *joined and knit together by what every joint supplies, according to the effective working by which every part does its share* (Eph. 4:16).

Lee Iacocca once asked legendary football coach Vince Lombardi what it took to make a winning team. Lombardi's answer is told in the book *Iacocca:*

> There are a lot of coaches with good ball clubs who know the fundamentals and have plenty of discipline but still don't win the game. Then you come to the third ingredient: If you're going to play together as a team, you've got to care for each other. You've got to love each other. Each player has to be thinking about the next guy and saying to himself: "If I don't block that man, Paul is going to get his legs broken. I have to do my job well in order that he can do his." The difference between mediocrity and greatness is the feeling these guys have for each other *(Toler 1998, 63).*

Former University of South Carolina football coach Lou Holtz gave one of the best descriptions of this quality. Lou explained that he once watched a television program that examined why some men and women were willing to die for their country. The program, profiling the United

States Marines, the French Foreign Legion, and the British Commandos, determined that people were willing to die for their country because of the love they had for their fellow human beings. One of those interviewed was a soldier who had been wounded in combat and was recovering in a hospital when he heard that his unit was going back out on a dangerous mission. The soldier escaped from the hospital and went with them, only to be wounded again. When asked why he did it, he said, "After you live and work with people, you soon realize that your survival depends upon them." Now that's teamwork!

As Christians, our hearts are "knit together in love" (Col. 2:2). As it relates to Christianity, such bonding is not a luxury but a necessity: *Teams that don't bond can't build!*

The Coaching Paradigm

Today's Christian leaders can learn much from the example of successful sports coaches. Effective coaches develop their teams through:

- Recruiting and building winning relationships
- Focusing on training the players
- Giving and receiving feedback
- Monitoring performance
- Motivating the players to win

It is remarkable how these same principles are reflected in the great leaders of the Bible. Consider, for example, the effectiveness Barnabas had in motivating the new converts to remain true to the Lord:

> And the hand of the Lord was with them, and a great number believed and turned to the Lord. Then news of these things came to the ears of the church in Jerusalem, and they sent out Barnabas to go as far as Antioch. When he came and had seen the grace of God, he was glad, and encouraged them all that with

purpose of heart they should continue with the Lord. For he was a good man, full of the Holy Spirit and of faith. And a great many people were added to the Lord *(Acts 11:21-24).*

Likewise, Paul exemplified an extraordinary ability to mold diverse people into a cohesive team. His team was truly a "multinational force," made up of disciples from various countries and continents: *Sopater of Berea accompanied him to Asia—also Aristarchus and Secundus of the Thessalonians, and Gaius of Derbe, and Timothy, and Tychicus and Trophimus of Asia* (20:4).

The Dream Team Can Be Yours!

A few years ago, the United States Olympic basketball team was referred to as the Dream Team. Comprised of players such as Michael Jordan, Larry Bird, Magic Johnson, Charles Barkley, and other greats, the U.S. team seemed invincible. The team was such an assembly of stars that even the players on opposing teams seemed awestruck, often asking the Dream Team for autographs. These NBA stars modeled teamwork. They set aside their personal stardom to perform as a unit.

Every coach fantasizes about having a team like the Dream Team. But even the Dream Team would have failed if the players had not set aside their personal goals and focused on group goals. A team of average players might very well be stronger than a team of stars if the members of the star team refuse to blend their talents with those of fellow players. Therefore, the strength of the team is not based solely on the skill of individual players. The more bonded and the more centrally focused the team, the stronger that team will be.

This is good news to a pastor who looks across his or her congregation and sees a group of "average" laypersons.

Believe it or not, the pastor-coach and those "average" people can pull together in an astounding way to produce ministry teams that excel the efforts of any basketball Dream Team.

Embracing the Dream

Researcher George Barna recently predicted that 40 percent of those presently pastoring will be out of the ministry within 10 years. A ministry shift is needed to share the pastoral workload, avoid professional burnout, and keep the church on track. I believe that the answer is in the "coaching" model. But beware: Paradigm shifts are never easy. Before you attempt to radically shift the leadership philosophy of your church, ask yourself these questions:

- Am I growing as a leader?
- Is my church willing to grow?
- Where do I start making changes?
- What should remain the same?
- Who will lead the change?

If the "coaching" concept seems a logical answer to these questions, then the time has come to consider the change. Moving from a traditional structure to a "coaching" model takes courage and perseverance—but it is worth the effort. And besides that, nothing worth doing is entirely risk-free.

The Bible describes several instances of paradigm shifts, but perhaps none more dramatically than the outpouring of the Holy Spirit on the Day of Pentecost in Acts 2:

> So they were all amazed and perplexed, saying to one another, "Whatever could this mean?" Others mocking said, "They are full of new wine" But Peter, standing up with the eleven, raised his voice and said to them, "Men of Judea and all who dwell in Jerusalem, let this be known to you, and heed my words. For

these are not drunk, as you suppose, since it is only the third hour of the day. But this is what was spoken by the prophet Joel: 'And it shall come to pass in the last days, says God, that I will pour out of My Spirit on all flesh; your sons and your daughters shall prophesy, your young men shall see visions, your old men shall dream dreams. And on My menservants and on My maidservants I will pour out My Spirit in those days; and they shall prophesy'" *(vv. 12-18).*

Peter's proclamation signaled the end of the old religious system and the beginning of the new. But the church at Jerusalem struggled with how to handle this change, as seen by the questions raised at the apostolic council meeting in Acts 15. The new ministry model seemed to be much easier for the church at Antioch and other churches that were not as deeply entrenched in the old system of religious life.

The Members of Your Dream Team

After you make the decision to shift your ministry emphasis to being a pastor-coach, you'll need to surround yourself with "team members" who will catch your vision and carry out your game plans. You can recruit your own dream team to get the job done.

Joseph Garlington Sr. taught about recruiting such a team in his article "David's Dream Team," published in *Worship Leader* (March-April 1998). Pointing to the Scripture setting in 1 Chron. 12—14, Garlington said he liked the parallels between David's team and the pastor's team—both "ministering together, fulfilling a shared destiny." There are some highly relevant characteristics between David's team and the dream team you may want to assemble for your ministry:

They fellowshipped with him in his sufferings. *They could see the destiny before they saw success.* David was relatively unknown, but he had such an obvious mission that his team was willing to drop their previous plans and follow him. They were willing to go through the adversity of David's growth to prominence.

You don't have to be well known to form your dream team. You simply need a sense of Spirit-led mission, a love for people, a desire to build them up in their ministries, and a perseverance to stay with the task. Those qualities will attract team members to your cause.

They were equipped and skilled. *They brought their weapons and abilities to David for his use.* As had already been mentioned, God has gifted laypersons with abilities that can be developed and utilized. The pastor-coach doesn't have to gift the team—they are already gifted. There are dream team members sitting in your congregation waiting for a call to action.

They were in shape. *They maintained a fitness level that kept them competitive.* In your search for dream team members, don't overlook the more mature saints. The rising population of baby boomers in the church is a source of strength. The skills, maturity, experience, and spirituality of those who have walked with the Lord for longer periods of time are a great *plus* for recruiting them to ministry teams.

They were men of peace. *They had no hidden agendas, no desire to betray.* One of the key qualities you must look for in your recruiting process is loyalty. People who are faithful in their church attendance, in their giving, and in their personal relationships probably possess those characteristics that will make them loyal to your team ministry as well.

They had a heart relationship with David. *These were men who wanted to be "knit" to David's heart, uniting with him in his desire to establish the kingdom.* Hollywood calls it "chemistry"—actors have such an affinity for each other that it comes through on the screen. If you don't feel a "connection" to a recruit, that person may not be the one you need on your team. Jesus was certainly connected to His disciples!

They were joined by revelation. *They were clear about their reasons for being part of his team.* Pastor-coaches should avoid "warm body" recruiting. Putting someone on a team just because you need another person for the team can be devastating. Why does your recruit want to be on the team? Is it because of guilt? Does he or she simply want a place of prominence in the church? Think about the motivations before asking someone to serve on your team.

They were entrusted with responsibility. *When he realized their desire to help him fulfill his destiny, he could confidently delegate to them significant areas of responsibility.* I've already mentioned the necessity of turning responsibility over to laypersons through ministry teams. Ministry team members need to understand that you are depending on them—that they are an integral part of the ministry. They need to be assured that you just couldn't get by without their help. **Their feeling of importance will determine their level of performance!**

They understood the times. *They were politically astute and in touch with the issues of the times.* Dream team members don't have their heads buried in the sands. And, the pastor-coach can keep them updated by integrating current event issues into their training times. The pastor-coach has a responsibility to make the church ministry relevant.

They were able to stay in battle formation. *They were "submitted" once the assignments were made.* Haywood Cosby writes of his boyhood experiences on the farm and the different "styles" of the two family cows on his farm. One was trustworthy and gentle, always waiting for him at the gate. He said she didn't need a fence. She would head for the barn at milking time without any encouragement. The other

Success is being where God places you, doing what God wants you to do, with the gifts He has given you.

—Larry Gilbert

cow was just the opposite. Cosby would always have to go looking for her. She would be the one to jump over the fence and stray from the farm. Sometimes she was so belligerent that Cosby would have to tie her up to milk her (see *Pulpit Helps*, February 1999).

Some of your church ministry personnel fall into the first category—docile, dependable, trustworthy. Others need fences. Dream team members usually don't need a fence. They will be "waiting at the gate" to do the work of ministry.

Creating Gifted Team Members

In the boxing film classic *Rocky*, boxer Rocky Balboa sums up the power of teamwork and synergy as he describes the relationship between him and his girlfriend: "I've got gaps. She's got gaps. But together we've got no gaps."

That is God's intention for the church: individuals molded together in such a way that their unique gifts and callings form a "gapless," functional organism. But such cohesiveness is not easy or automatic. Rocky and his girlfriend had something special that they had worked hard to develop.

Many leaders say a hearty "Amen" when they hear about ministry "coaching," but then fall short when it comes to implementing the needed changes. There are several critical steps that a leader must take if a shift to a team ministry/coaching model is to be successful.

Educate the laity. Dick Iverson says in his book *Team Ministry*, "The congregation must be educated by a slow, patient, and thorough teaching process." The teaching process might include a series of sermons on the biblical imperatives of a coaching concept and how that will involve the specific gifts of the laity. Of course, there must first be an emphasis on the significance of the spiritual gifts themselves. Even if laypersons know *what* their spiritual gifts are, many of them do not see *how* their spiritual gift *relates* to their lives, how it *relates* to other people's lives, how it *relates* to the local church, or how it *relates* to the Body of Christ as a whole. Helping people discover their spiritual gift without teaching them *what* a spiritual gift is, is like giving someone a new appliance without providing the operator's manual. They will never fully understand it. There are nine identifying marks of a spiritual gift:

- The hands of God
- A supernatural capacity
- A supernatural desire
- Our tools for doing the work of the ministry
- A source of joy in a Christian's life
- A divine motivator
- A divine influence on motives
- A divine calling and responsibility
- The building blocks of the church

Motivate the laity. One of the key elements in motivating people is the level of motivation manifested by their leader. For example, if the pastor is highly motivated, that energy will spill over onto the laity. They will soon be as excited as the pastor, and the wheels of innovation will begin to turn. This type of motivation does not need to be "worked at." It's a natural spreading of an eager flame, ready to ignite everyone it touches. It's the kind of motivation the apostles expressed on the Day of Pentecost. Once pastors discover *their own God-inspired vision* of what the "coaching" approach can do for their church, a motivated laity will usually follow.

In one sense, every Christian is *already* motivated, since every Christian has a spiritual gift. Accompanying that spiritual is a supernatural, internal motivation from God to utilize the gift. Once realized, action begins to take place without the necessity of outside motivation and prompting. In fact, it is the Holy Spirit himself who motivates that person from within.

Train the laity. The main element in training the laity involves two important factors. First, they must be educated in the Eph. 4 method of pastoring. If laypersons aren't "retrained" to function under such a pastor, they might easily become disheartened by what they perceive as the pastor's lack of fulfilling a "traditional role." Second, they must be trained to recognize their own spiritual gifts and to understand how those gifts can be used within the Body of Christ, that is, on which Ministry Action Team they will function best. As has been said, this training can occur as a special series of Sunday night classes or by encouraging them to read a book on team ministry, such as this one.

> *Do not withhold good from those to whom it is due, when it is in the power of your hand to do so.*
>
> —Prov. 3:27

Empower the laity. After individual spiritual gifts have been determined and ministry teams have been established, those teams should not have to wait for church board approval for each specific action. The teams should be given a budget (and the freedom) to make necessary plans and decisions. Empowered people feel:

- They can make a difference.
- They are responsible for results.
- They have control over their assignments.
- They are part of the team.

Determining Spiritual Gifts

Building an effective team depends on putting the right people in the right places. The best way to determine in what place each layperson belongs is to determine his or her spiritual gifts. Unfortunately we have been conditioned to believe that a person must struggle for years in the "School of Hard Knocks" to discover his or her spiritual gifts. *Most laypeople will die never knowing what their spiritual gifts actually were!*

Some Christian workers give testimonies of how it took them as long as 20 years to "come to the conclusion" that God had given them certain gifts. Conditioning of this kind discourages many people from even wanting to tackle such an "overwhelming task." Although it may take some time to find and develop spiritual gifts, there are seven action steps that must be a part of the process.

Step 1: Pray for God's direction. Laypersons should be encouraged to ask God to reveal their spiritual gifts to them—waiting on God until they are *sure* they understand what those gifts are. That will take more than "Now I lay me down to sleep" praying. Older saints used to call it "praying through." It means waiting on God in times of Bible study and prayer until the answer comes to your spirit. Our Heavenly Father has no intention of keeping us in a state of confusion about His will for our lives. He wants us to know where we fit into His Master Plan.

Step 2: Study the characteristics of spiritual gifts. Materials such as Larry Gilbert's book *Team Ministry: How to Find Meaning and Fulfillment Through Understanding the Spiritual Gift Within You* (Ephesians Four Ministries) along with the *Team Ministry Spiritual Gifts Inventory* will help laypersons determine their gifts. Also, Dan Reiland, with *Injoy Group,* has designed a gift discovery inventory that will help laypersons discover their major spiritual gifts.

Step 3: Seek the help of a more mature Christian. (This should be someone *who has been educated on the principles and uses of spiritual gifts.*) A lot of people who are willing to help with spiritual gift education have only a superficial awareness themselves about what spiritual gifts are. Be certain that the Christians you seek help from are indeed "mentors"—people who are able to evaluate and teach based on their "recognized" love for the Lord and service to Him.

Step 4: Admit that there are gifts you don't have. After prayer and Bible study, and consulting with Christian mentors, most people will recognize that there are some gifts they do *not* possess. While it is good to recognize the value of all the gifts, laypersons should understand that God "gifts" them based on their uniqueness and their areas of ministry. For example, it would be a very confusing worship service if everyone had the gift of "exhortation." There wouldn't be any listeners. Nobody would be available to usher—and the coffee and doughnuts wouldn't be on the table in the fellowship hall.

Step 5: List at least three gifts that you might already have. Some teach that people have only one spiritual gift. This view is often based on the word "the" in 2 Tim. 1:6, where Paul says to *stir up* the *gift of God which is in you.* While another may quote 1 Cor. 7:7 (KJV), *Every man hath his proper gift of God, one after this manner, and another after that.* The word "proper" refers to a dominant gift, while other gifts may also be present.

Step 6: Begin to function on a Ministry Action Team. Apart from God's revelation, this is the most important principle in determining a gift. Laypersons should be encouraged to utilize those gifts revealed in their evaluation. If possible, have newcomers begin as helpers, because a layperson who misinterprets his or her gift will easily become discouraged.

Step 7: Look for personal fulfillment and positive results. If people don't enjoy what they are doing, it may be an indication that they are not in the will of God! Remind your people that God did not call us to a *life of misery* but to a *life of fulfilling ministry*. Serving the Lord is not supposed to be a "grin and bear it" proposition. He does not call us to a life of drudgery, serving in areas that will never bring fulfillment. He calls us to delightful duty. God wants us to live a fulfilled life, and our spiritual gifts should be a source of joy as we serve Him.

The Role of Spiritual Gifts in Teamwork

In his book *Team Spirituality,* William J. Carter says these principles of spiritual gifts discovery need constant repetition:

"We do not always know why God calls those whom He calls." When there is "spiritual innovation" in ministry, members of the old school may not recognize "paradigm pioneers," or the meaning of their call from God.

"God sometimes equips us after He calls us. He does

Team-Building Axioms

1. Staff recruitment and development should be in response to the mission of the Body.
2. Faith and a willingness to grow in its practice are a necessity for all who work in the Body.
3. Persons chosen for staff positions must possess and be able to exhibit gifts of ministry consistent with the mission of the Body.
4. Competence in the gifts of ministry is more important than conformity with traditional norms.
5. Good interpersonal relationships are vital to effective performance and to spiritual growth.
6. Members of a church staff should work together, alongside one another, in the performance of ministry.
7. The Body of Christ is constructed of the gifts of its members, and nothing else can replace these building blocks.

8. The basic task of the designated leadership is to discover the gifts of the members of the Body and provide them arenas for expression.
9. The ministry of any congregation is a continuous expression of the will of God, and each part has equal value with all the others: paid or volunteer, ordained or unordained.
10. Ministry is always an expression of the particular gifts of the individual within the general context of the mission of the Body (*Carter 1997, 118-19*).

not just call the obviously equipped." There are times when we confuse "skills" and "gifts," believing all of us will be called to do what we do best. But gifts are more comprehensive than skills, and not as easy to define.

Recognizing Different Styles Among the Team Members

Not only will each team member bring different spiritual gifts to the team, but also each will have a different style of participation. Glenn M. Parker points to four different types of team members, each contributing in a different way to the success of the team:

A **Contributor** is a *task-oriented* team member who enjoys providing the team with good technical information and data. Such members "do their homework" and push the team to set high performance standards and use their resources wisely. (**Key words:** dependable, responsible, organized, efficient, logical, clear, relevant, pragmatic, systematic, proficient.)

A **Collaborator** is a *goal-directed* team member who sees the vision, mission, or goal of the team as paramount. Such team members are flexible and open to the new ideas and are willing to pitch in and work outside their defined role, as well as to share the limelight with others. (**Key** *words:* cooperative, flexible, confident, forward-looking, conceptual, accommodating, generous, open, visionary, imaginative.)

A **Communicator** is a *process-oriented* team member who is an effective listener and facilitator of involvement, conflict resolution, consensus building, feedback, and the creation of an informal, relaxed climate. (**Key words:** supportive, encouraging, relaxed, tactful, helpful, friendly, patient, informal, considerate, spontaneous).

A **Challenger** is a team member who questions the goals, methods, and even the ethics of the team. Such members are willing to disagree with the leader or higher authority and to encourage the team to take well-conceived risks. (**Key words:** candid, ethical, questioning, honest, outspoken, principled, adventurous, aboveboard, and brave.)

Expect some of your team members to need direction, some to need coaching, some to need support, and others to be ready for you to delegate responsibility to. That is what the "coach" and the team leaders are for. A pastor-coach will drown in discouragement if expectations are set too high for implementing Ministry Action Teams. There will be those team members who don't seem as motivated or as "connected" with the whole team concept. That is normal. But watching those laypersons grow into team members to whom you can delegate responsibility is one of the greatest joys of coaching.

In his book *The Power Behind Positive Thinking* (San Francisco: Harper), Eric Fellem writes about the baseball summer of '61 when Roger Maris and Mickey Mantle battled for the home-run crown. Although Mantle hit a lot of home runs, he also had a lot of strikeouts. When questioned about the strikeouts, Mickey Mantle replied, "Look, fellas. Every batter knows he's going to strike out so many times every week. I just go up there and do my best, and if I strike out, I know that's one down for this week and I'm just that much closer to a hit or a homer." Encourage your team members that a strikeout is a prelude to a homer!

Putting the Gifts in Action

It is not enough for believers to just learn about their spiritual gifts. They must utilize (and develop) them. God did not give spiritual gifts as "badges" to be pinned on His children so they could brag, "I am a teacher," "I am a server," or "I am an exhorter." He intended them to be used in the ministry of the gospel.

In order to use gifts to the fullest, they must be continuously developed. For many years I (Gilbert), like many others, taught that there are three phases of spiritual gifts: (1) discover or recognize; (2) develop; and (3) use the gift. But now I see that I was guilty of not telling people *how* to develop and *how* to use the gifts they had. The proper procedure is this: (1) discover or recognize; (2) use; and (3) develop. *Laypersons develop their gifts only as they use them.*

As believers function using their spiritual gifts, they are developing those gifts in the process. For example, rather than spending all your time "studying" a spiritual gift, it would be more advisable to spend that time "practicing" that gift in ministry. So by functioning as an exhorter, people with the gift of exhortation will learn more about exhorting and be able to teach others. As a result, they will naturally want to attend seminars, read books, listen to tapes, and take advantage of other educational opportunities concerning that particular area of ministry. By doing these things, they will expand their gift of exhortation. Likewise with other gifts; administrators will learn new management techniques not just by studying about management but by practicing those techniques.

As believers utilize their gifts within the framework of

ministry, they are actually expanding the capacity, motivation, and characteristics of that gift. In other words, as laypersons develop the *ministry*, they develop their *gifts* for ministry.

DISCOVERY + USE = DEVELOPMENT

Spiritual gifts are provisions given by the Holy Spirit to minister *to* people and *through* people (see 1 Cor. 12:25). Exhort your congregation to seriously consider the importance of this concept, for only through the *use* of their spiritual gifts can believers truly minister to one another as well as to a world that needs Christ.

Team-Building Tips

- Establish a plan for spiritual growth among team leaders.
- Involve the team in setting goals and standards.
- Create listening posts.
- Accentuate the positive!
- Make teamwork fun.
- Improve ministry team morale by celebrating the small victories.
- Value team-member differences.
- Welcome new teammates enthusiastically.
- Coach or guide constructively when a mistake is made.
- Create symbols of team success.
- Praise loudly and blame softly.
- Conduct exit interviews when a team member leaves.

4

Establishing Ministry Action Teams in the Local Church

The body is not one member but many.
(1 Cor. 12:14)

"Down, Set, Wait!" Making Ministry Adjustments

ANYONE WHO HAS WATCHED a professional football game has seen this. The quarterback lines up behind the center, looks to the left and to the right at his linemen, begins the cadence, "Down, set, . . ." And then suddenly he calls a time-out. What's wrong? The quarterback has taken a look at the defense of the opposing team, and then looked at the formation of his offense. Something isn't right. An adjustment needs to be made before play continues.

Behind that quarterback's decision is the experience and training of the coach. On any professional football team, the coach has spent years preparing for the task at hand and knows football inside out. Even though the coach isn't the one to snap the ball, the coach is the mastermind behind that action and the whole game. The coach is the one who has educated the team and taught them the methods by which they can win the game.

The same is true of the pastor-coach. Before he or she expects laypersons to become a collection of gifted ministry teams, solid education must take place.

For a church to grow, it must be healthy. A healthy church meets the needs of its members and reaches out to the community it serves. A healthy church is balanced, as Paul spells out in Eph. 4:16: *From whom the whole body fitly joined together and compacted by that which every joint supplieth, according to the effectual working in the measure of every part, maketh increase of the body unto the edifying of itself in love* (KJV). A healthy church is increasing (growing in numbers by reaching people for Christ) and *edifying* itself (ministering to the needs within its own body). A healthy church ministers both *to* the body and *outside* the body. A healthy church balances its ministry with the gifts God has given it.

People's Needs and God's Provisions

I (Gilbert) was young and had never taught before, nor had I received any training as a teacher. But I started teaching an adult Sunday School class. However, I realized that if I was going to be successful, not only did I need to teach certain material, but also I had to meet definite needs in the lives of my students. My classes didn't always go the way I had hoped. Whenever I bombed out, being an analytical person, I always asked the question, *Why didn't it work?*

I really wanted to do it right, so I headed to the Christian bookstore to buy a book on being a more effective communicator. My studies reinforced that if I was going to minister and reach people, I had to meet certain needs in their lives—not just one or two needs but several needs—in order to effectively minister to the whole person.

Later, through an in-depth study of spiritual gifts, I was amazed as God pointed out to me the correlation between these needs and the spiritual gifts. The characteristics of each gift met a need that was evident. The more I studied, the more I could see how they dovetailed perfectly. On one

```
┌─────────────────────────────────────────────────────┐
│                                                       │
│                   Team Ministry                       │
│                                                       │
│      PEOPLE'S NEEDS              GOD'S PROVISIONS      │
│                                                       │
│    1. Salvation               2. the EVANGELISTS      │
│    3. Awareness of Sin    21.  4. the PROPHETS        │
│    5. Doctrine            to   6. the TEACHERS         │
│    7. To Know How        serve 8. the EXHORTERS        │
│    9. Shepherding       others 10. PASTOR/SHEPHERDS    │
│   11. Comforting              12. MERCY SHOW-ERS       │
│   13. A Helping Hand          14. the SERVERS         │
│   15. Financial Aid           16. the GIVERS          │
│   17. Leadership              18. ADMINISTRATORS       │
│   19. Fellowship              20. the ENTIRE BODY      │
│   22. A Mature Christian      23. the "TEAM"          │
│              24. "LASTING GROWTH"                     │
│                                                       │
└─────────────────────────────────────────────────────┘
```

side were the needs of the people that had to be met, and on the other side were the gifts with dominant characteristics that would minister to the needs.

The above chart is the result of that study. The left side lists the needs that the church must meet in a person's life if he or she is to mature as a Christian. The other side of the chart is the gift that predominantly ministers to that particular need.

Let's look at the needs one at a time and see how God has equipped the church to minister to them. (The numbering system will help you follow the chart.)

No. 1: The people's first need is *salvation.* Rom. 3:23 says, *For all have sinned and fall short of the glory of God.*

Which team member meets this need in a person's life? The *evangelist* **(No. 2).** This is not to say the evangelist is the only person in a church to lead people to a saving knowledge of Jesus Christ. But, if you took a poll, you would see that the evangelist is probably the one who has reached 80 or 90 percent of the converts. Evangelists are salespeople for Christ. They are aggressive and confrontational.

Confrontational evangelists (called "soul winners" by some) try to motivate others to reach out to lost people. They give testimonies like, "I went on a plane trip and happened to sit next to a guy who wasn't saved." They end the story by saying, "As the plane touched down, the gentleman beside me bowed his head and accepted Christ as his Savior." They get on an elevator with a "sinner" on the 6th floor and get off on the 12th floor with a "saint." Again, I need to stress that those with the gift of evangelism are not the only ones who can lead people to Christ. But they lead more people to the point of decision, even though someone else may have influenced the people and laid the groundwork for their decision to accept Christ.

It is crucial to understand the responsibility of the evangelist versus the responsibility of all Christians to witness. This distinction is so great that I wrote a complete book on the subject, *Team Evangelism: How to Influence Your Loved Ones for Christ When You Don't Have the Gift of Evangelism.*

No. 3 is the people's need to have an **awareness of sin.** Someone once said that the world is so *churchy* and the church is so *worldly* that we can't tell the difference. The world has so much influence on us, even as Christians, that we sometimes have a hard time recognizing sin. The person who meets this need in our Christian life is the **prophet (No. 4).**

Prophets tell the Word of God like it is. They can see what's wrong in people's lives and point out what's wrong in a church, but their weakness is that they often don't have the ability to see what is *right* about people. Their ministry mostly manifests itself through preaching, and usually that consists largely of pointing out sin. They do what we think of as *hard* preaching. They usually get excited, step on toes, and preach for conviction. Their preaching will stir your heart and sometimes make you mad. They are typically the hellfire-and-brimstone type preachers.

No. 5 is a people's need to know **doctrine**, or *the principles for right living*. Only the Word of God can truly tell us what is right. The person who meets this need is the **teacher (No. 6).** *Didasko* is the Greek word that means "to teach": to communicate knowledge, to relay facts, or to make known. Teachers are always studying and communicating the norms, standards, and doctrines of Scripture to others, verbally and through the written page.

No. 7 is the people's need **to know "how."** The person who meets that need is the **exhorter (No. 8).** Exhorters spend their time teaching people how to do things. They also motivate and excite people, enabling them to get more done. They make great counselors, because they tend to provide practical solutions to problems.

No. 9 is the people's need to be **shepherded,** or *cared for*. Who meets that need? The **pastor-shepherd (No. 10).** Shepherds have a caretaker approach to leadership. They are burdened to teach the Word of God and to care for the people around them. They protect and shelter their sheep. This gift is not limited to the position of senior pastor. *Many* Christians have the gift of shepherding, especially women. It can be used in a variety of positions inside and outside the church, from Sunday School teachers to den mothers.

No. 11 is the people's need to be **comforted.** Who will meet that need? The **mercy show-er (No. 12).** Mercy show-ers are usually soft-spoken but outgoing people who seem to always know what to say or what not to say when we hurt. They empathize with people, feeling their hurts and joys, rather than just having sympathy for them.

If a tragedy were to happen in your life, you would appreciate a visit or call from the person with the gift of show-ing mercy, because he or she would help you deal with pain better. Mercy show-ers provide a special support that oth-ers don't. They attract people who are hurting, because they have the ability to put themselves in someone else's shoes. They also attract people who are experiencing times of joy. People like to share their happy days with them as well, because mercy show-ers rejoice with them.

No. 13 is the people's need for a ***helping hand***. In or-der to keep a church building from falling down, people who are willing to do the maintenance and take care of the build-ing are needed. The ***server* (No. 14)** is the person who meets that need because the server is very content doing the physical labor around the church, and many times at your house as well. Servers get fulfillment out of doing what many people see as menial tasks. They are content working behind the scenes. They don't need or like the spotlight on them. They are not kings but king-makers. It's a gift that God has given to many believers.

No. 15 is the people's need for ***financial aid***. Finances are needed to support the ministries and the missions in the church as we meet people's physical needs. The person who meets this need is the ***giver* (No. 16).** Givers are very mis-sion-minded. It's not unusual to see a church that has sever-al givers in it, supporting many mission projects. While all Christians have the responsibility to tithe, God has given some the ability to give far beyond their tithe.

Many people with the gift of giving have the ability to make money, but not always. They usually like to keep their giving private and don't seek recognition. They are blessed by helping others in need and supporting special projects and ministries of the church. They are good stewards and want to know that their money is being put to good use.

"Giving" and "serving" are two gifts the church really

needs to place an extra emphasis on today, because we've allowed the government to take over in these areas. We give to churches to add a wing on the church building, but when it comes to giving to an individual Christian, we rarely do that anymore. We've allowed the government to make up for our failure as believers to do what is right.

When a person in the church has financial problems, Christians usually say something like, "Can you borrow the money someplace to get this straightened out?" or, "Surely there is some type of welfare program that will help" or, "You can have the money if you sign a note and pay it back monthly—with interest." We're telling people to go somewhere else, when God says in Rom. 12:13, that the church in team ministry should meet those needs in people's lives, *Distributing to the needs of the saints* and being *given to hospitality*. (See also Acts 6.)

No. 17 is the people's need for ***leadership***. Most people are followers. In order to reach a goal, 84 percent of the people need a totally planned, supervised program. If the program is carefully laid out, 14 percent of the people are able to meet that goal with little supervision. However, only 2 percent of the people can create a dream and carry it through to completion by themselves. These latter people are ***administrators*** **(No. 18).** They are the leaders.

No. 19 is the people's need for ***fellowship***. Who meets this need? The ***entire body*** **(No. 20)** does. This includes all the *administrators, servers, givers, exhorters, prophets, teachers, evangelists, mercy show-ers,* and *pastor-shepherds*. All these gifted Christians combined, the entire church, must meet the people's need for fellowship. Polls have shown that most people who start attending a certain church do so for the fellowship they enjoy. We go to church to be with our friends.

No. 21 (running up the center of the chart) is the "catalyst" need—the people's need to *serve others*. The "catalyst need" ties together the whole array of spiritual gifts with the needs that must be met. *Humankind needs to serve others*. It's a need put in the heart of Christian and non-Christian alike by God himself. It's people wrapping their lives up in the lives of others. Anywhere that happens, you'll see happier, more contented, and less troubled people—simply because they are meeting a God-given need. As Christians, we need to serve others by ministering through our spiritual gifts. The most miserable people I know are selfish people, concerned only with themselves and their own welfare. They're miserable (and they make everyone around them just as miserable as they are).

Look at **No. 22** on the chart. If we look at the left side of the chart as if it were a math problem, what would we get by adding it all up? *A mature Christian*. After you have met all these needs in people's lives, they become mature. For every need we fail to meet, the people will be that much less mature. But, the closer we come to meeting all the needs, the more mature the individuals will become.

Tragically though, many churches miss one, two, three, or even all of the top four needs. To keep from making this mistake, we need to understand the *biblical procedure* for training Christians.

Second Tim. 3:16 states, *All Scripture is given by inspiration of God, and is profitable [for four things] for doctrine, for reproof, for correction, for instruction in righteousness.* We usually quote this scripture to support the inerrancy of the Bible. But let's look again and see the biblical procedure for training Christians. *First*, doctrine; *second*, reproof; *third*, correction; and *fourth*, instruction. I don't think it is any accident that Paul lists these four items in this order:

Doctrine refers to the norms and standards of the Scriptures. It constitutes the standards by which we must govern our lives and our ministries. Doctrine is

not the process of teaching but the product of teaching.
Reproof means to show what is wrong.
Correction involves showing what is right.
Instruction is simply how-to information and practical application.

Notice how these relate to the spiritual gifts. First, the main ministry of the *prophet* is pointing out *what is wrong*, while the main emphasis of the *teacher* is pointing out *what is right*. The primary ministry of the *exhorter* is simply telling *how to do it*.

We have a tendency to ignore some of these people, most often the prophet. After all, who wants someone stepping on his or her toes and pointing out what's wrong? The prophet makes us uncomfortable. In turn, we keep those who make us uncomfortable out of our lives.

Many churches lack a gifted teacher and a sound doctrinal foundation for their ministry. The person who is doctrine-oriented is usually fact-oriented rather than practical-application oriented. For that reason, even an outstanding teacher—teaching theology, doctrine, and prophecy week in and week out but without giving much practical application—will have a frustrated congregation.

In addition to doctrine, people need simple, practical, how-to teaching. For instance, consider the man who says, "I know I am coming up short as a father, but I'm tired of people telling me what I'm doing wrong. I want somebody to show me *how to* become a better father." On the other hand, you can't teach a man how to be a better father if he doesn't first feel convicted that he needs to be a better father. Without conviction, practical teaching will go in one ear and out the other. At the same time, the practical teacher can't be effective if his or her teaching is not based on proper theology, which comes from the gifted teacher.

Some teachers can both bring conviction and explain

how-to. Besides teaching, they have the secondary gift of exhortation or prophecy. However, the prophet is usually the one who gets us stirred up or convicted, and the practical exhorter is the one who comes in and gives us the how-to. This type of situation further emphasizes the balance and cooperation that the Bible describes when it deals with spiritual gifts.

Team ministry does not mean exclusiveness. Example: A man comes into your church for help and the secretary asks, "Are you saved?" He says, "No." So she says, "In that case, you first need to go to the end of the hall and see *Rev. Evangelist* so he can lead you to Christ. Then you need to go across the hall to see *Dr. Teacher* so he can show you what's right. After that, you should go upstairs and let *Counselor Exhorter* show you how to solve your problems." Team ministry involves people who will excel in these different areas of the ministry because of their God-given gifts, but there will always be some overlap in all the areas of giftedness and ministry.

When the right side of the chart is added together, it totals the **TEAM (No. 23).** The TEAM is a group of Christians empowered by the Holy Spirit. No doubt about it, this is the most powerful force on earth. For years we have let this awesome force lie nearly dormant. Although we have the most powerful force on earth, by doing nothing with it we're letting the world and humanism take over our schools, our government, and the news and entertainment media. As said by Edmund Burke, "All it takes for evil to triumph is for good men to do nothing."

No. 24 is the real bottom line. When you add all these met needs and active gifts together, you get ***lasting growth***. However, for lasting growth, the church has to meet *all* these needs in the members' lives. When you miss some of these needs, people are left incomplete. They subconsciously try to fulfill the missing needs. In many cases, they're not even aware the needs exist. All they know is that there's an emptiness in their lives, and they just move on, looking for another church that can meet their needs.

After moving through several churches, such people sometimes drop out completely, thinking that no church can meet their needs. Of course, very few churches can minister perfectly to *all* these needs. Yet the more needs are met, the more effective the church will be in lasting growth.

The Balance Needed for a Healthy Church

Some churches are strong on outreach. But even though they are getting people saved, many of these converts are simply going out the back door because of an ineffective follow-up program. On the other hand, some churches have good teaching ministries but don't evangelize. The idea is to achieve balance. The balanced church is a growing and healthy church.

In three places where Paul writes on spiritual gifts (Rom. 12; 1 Cor. 12; and Eph. 4), he uses a five-way analogy of (1) the human body, (2) the Body of Christ, (3) the church, and (4) the members that have (5) spiritual gifts. The church is compared to the human body. Members with the various spiritual gifts are compared to the parts of the body. First Cor. 12:12-22 says:

> For as the body is one, and hath many members, and all the members of that one body, being many, are one body: so also is Christ . . . For the body is not one member, but many. If the foot shall say, Because I am not the hand, I am not of the body; is it therefore not of the body? . . . If the whole body were an eye, where were the hearing? If the whole were hearing, where were the smelling? But now hath God set the members every one of them in the body, as it hath pleased him . . . And the

eye cannot say unto the hand, I have no need of thee:
nor again the head to the feet, I have no need of you.
Nay, much more those members of the body, which
seem to be more feeble, are necessary *(KJV)*.

The question is, *When does the Body of Christ function
most effectively and efficiently?* When every member is doing
what it is supposed to do. When you write with your hands,
walk on your feet, hear with your ears, see with your eyes,
and all members are working together for one common
goal, you are balanced and can function efficiently.

Your responsibility, then, is to equip the laypersons to
exercise the spiritual gifts God has given them, in a *team* effort with the rest of the diversely gifted body, to meet all
the needs of every person possible. To develop this effective
team, all the gifts must be operating in one local church,
thus meeting the needs of all the people in that church or
community. We complement each other and meet each
other's needs; therefore, we make an effective *team*.

The "Little Toe" Principle

Some laypersons think, "I know that I'm part of the body,
but I'm just the little toe. I'm really not important. I don't have
much part in the body, and I'm not effective at all."

I know a man whose little toe was cut off in an accident. The little toe has much to do with the balance of the
body. If a layperson is the little toe in his or her church, he or
she has the same effect on the church (the Body of Christ)
as this man's little toe had on his body. That layperson is the
balance of the church.

The little toe really doesn't have any effective muscles
in it. If a person leans off balance and starts to fall, the little
toe has no muscles to stop the person from falling. But it immediately sends a signal to the brain that says "out of balance." Then the brain sends a signal to various other muscles

to contract to keep the person from falling. My friend without a little toe discovered that if he ran, walked too fast, or simply wasn't paying attention he'd lose his balance and fall.

The worst thing "little toe" laypersons can do is to fall asleep. The little toe that goes to sleep, just like the foot that goes to sleep, affects the whole body. If you have some "little toe" laypersons who have fallen asleep on the job, they could be part of what's holding back your church. Therefore as pastor-coach, make sure you communicate to each team member how much he or she is important to an effectively functioning Body.

According to Prov. 18:15, *The heart of the discerning acquires knowledge; the ears of the wise seek it out* (NIV). Modeling and encouraging continuing education is one of the key responsibilities of the senior pastor. Harold J. Westing states, "It's only logical that the church staff must model how a team is to function." Purchase good books for your leaders to read. Encourage them to listen to cassette tapes. Send them to seminars.

The more individual church members minister in their areas of gifting, the more balanced the church will be, the more lasting numerical and spiritual growth will take place, and the more God will be honored.

Now in the church that was at Antioch there were certain prophets and teachers: Barnabas, Simeon who was called Niger, Lucius of Cyrene, Manaen who had been brought up with Herod the tetrarch, and Saul. As they ministered to the Lord and fasted, the Holy Spirit said, "Now separate to Me Barnabas and Saul for the work to which I have called them." Then, hav-

> I have never heard anything about the resolutions of the disciples, but a great deal about the Acts of the Apostles.
> —Horace Mann

ing fasted and prayed, and laid hands on them, they sent them away *(Acts 13:1-3)*.

Oliver Wendell Holmes once wrote, "I find that the great thing is not so much where we stand as in what direction we are moving. To reach the port of heaven we must sail, sometimes with the wind and sometimes against it, but we must sail and not drift, nor lie at anchor."

We've talked about the importance of lay ministry teams. We've also seen the role of the pastor-coach in the success of the teams. But there comes a time when we must move from the strategy session to the playing field.

Marlene Wilson writes about moving to that playing field in her article *Turning Pewsitters into Players* (*Leadership*, fall 1996), "To get pewsitters moving, the pastor can do several things. *Interview new members* to discover their strengths and gifts. *Define leadership goals*. If members and potential leaders know what to expect in leadership roles, they won't be scared away by the fear of too little knowledge or too much responsibility. *Teach a team approach* that allows everyone to contribute their strengths and weakness, concerns and dreams. *Encourage natural leaders* while making sure that unnatural leaders aren't forced into leadership roles."

In an interview with David Frost, General Norman Schwarzkopf, the commander of the Allied forces in the Gulf War, was asked, "What's the greatest lesson you've learned out of all this?"

Schwarzkopf replied, "I think there is one really fundamental military truth. And that's that you can add up the correlation of forces, you can look at the number of tanks, you can look at the number of airplanes, you can look at all these factors of military might and put them together. But unless the soldier on the ground, or the airman in the air, has the will to win, has the strength of character to go into the battle, believes that his cause is just, and has the support of his country—all the rest of that stuff is irrelevant."

The same is true of church ministry teams. Without each person's conviction that the cause is worth the price, the battle will never be won, and the team will not succeed. There must be commitment. We must get the team onto the playing field!

However, a 1993 Gallup poll of religion in America found that 50 percent of church members are unwilling to do anything for the church, 40 percent are just waiting to be asked, and only 10 percent are presently involved in the church's ministry. Certainly these percentages will have to dramatically change if the church in America is going to have the impact God intends for it to have. Ministry Action Teams is the answer. It's time to include and empower the 40 percent who are waiting to be asked!

How to Ensure Successful Ministry Action Teams

When you have educated and gift-tested your congregation, you are free to begin establishing your Ministry Action Teams. But before the teams are fully established, the team members and the pastor-coach must understand the *four distinct phases* in a person's growth toward participation in the church's ministry:

1. *Assimilation.* In this phase a person comes to understand how to become a part of the local church.

2. *Teaching.* Those who are assimilated into the church need to be taught the biblical basis for lay ministry.

3. *Development.* Through gift testing and personality profiles, church members will begin to discover their spiritual gifts and callings.

4. *Placement.* The ultimate goal is for every member to become a minister in some capacity.

Not only must a church member grow from initial assimilation to actual placement in the church's ministry, the pastor's role must also "grow" through different phases. As the church grows, the pastor's hands-on ministry will *decrease*, while the congregation's hands-on ministry must *increase*. And, this hands-on ministry will be done most effectively by teams of people with *diverse knowledge and skills*, not by those who are just "clones" of the pastor.

Meeting the Needs of Team Members

In his book *Team Building: An Exercise in Leadership*, Robert B. Maddux lists seven things that a team member needs from the coach in order to be effective:

- A basic understanding of his or her job and its contribution to the team
- A continuing understanding of what is expected from him or her
- The opportunity to participate in planning change and to perform in keeping with team abilities
- The opportunity to receive assistance when needed
- Feedback to know how well he or she is doing
- Recognition and reward based on his or her performance
- The right work in a climate which encourages self-development (Maddux 1992, 11).

When institutions emerge, the focus tends to shift rather quickly from the movers and the movement to the machine and the monuments.

—Robert Dale

Not only must the "coach" firmly apply those principles in the establishment of the Ministry Action Teams, but also the team members themselves must embrace what I call "The Heavenly Seven."

The Heavenly Seven

1. Show love for one another.
2. Inform one another.
3. Learn as a group.
4. Acknowledge ministry gifts.
5. Have "the attitude of Christ."
6. Be committed to the cause of Christ.
7. Celebrate victories together.

Moving to the Ministry Action Team Philosophy

Anytime a church attempts a move from one ministry philosophy to another, some fundamental issues will be raised:

Issue No. 1: Inclusion—*Who is on the team?*

Issue No. 2: Direction—*Who is in charge?*

Issue No. 3: Affection—*How much trust is there?*

Issue No. 4: Implementation—*How will we achieve our goals?*

Building a team is not like making instant coffee; it is more of a "brewing" process. It takes time and requires patience by both the coach and the players. The process is not as blissful as some may lead you to believe. In fact, many churches have tried ministry teams and have seen them "stumble at the gate."

An effective Ministry Action Team, however, will view the growth process realistically. For example, in the initial year of shifting to Ministry Action Team activities, there is often a tentativeness. It is easy for discouragement and frustration to set in if only a few tangible results are seen right away. Understanding the following distinct stages of ministry team development and the possible "growing pains" inherent to each stage will help to head off discouragement.

Forming (getting organized for team ministry)

Storming (brainstorming, etc.)

Norming (establishing a consistent pattern of ministry)
Performing (working in the power of the Holy Spirit—
    tasks/ministry)

Now all who believed were together, and had all
things in common, and sold their possessions and
goods, and divided them among all, as anyone had
need. So continuing daily with one accord in the temple, and breaking bread from house to house, they ate
their food with gladness and simplicity of heart, praising
God and having favor with all the people. And the Lord
added to the church daily those who were being saved
(Acts 2:44-47).

The Seven Actions of Implementation

Implementing a team ministry involves seven distinct
actions:

- *Developing* the dream for Kingdom building
- *Structuring* the team for comprehensive ministry
- *Establishing* the role of each team leader
- *Communicating* vital information to the entire team

The Appointment of the Apostolic Team

*And He went up on the mountain and called to Him those
He Himself wanted. And they came to Him. Then He appointed twelve, that they might be with Him and that He might send
them out to preach, and to have power to heal sicknesses and
to cast out demons: Simon, to whom He gave the name Peter;
James the son of Zebedee and John the brother of James, to
whom He gave the name Boanerges, that is, "Sons of Thun-
der"; Andrew, Philip, Bartholomew, Matthew, Thomas, James
the son of Alphaeus, Thaddaeus, Simon the Canaanite; and Judas Iscariot, who also betrayed Him. And they went into a
house (Mark 3:13-19).*

- *Permitting* the team to innovate and create
- *Recognizing* the weaknesses inherent in all human beings
- *Releasing* the team to do ministry in Jesus' name

Launching Your Ministry Action Teams

Dodger great Tommy Lasorda once said, "My responsibility is to get my 25 guys playing for the name on the front of their uniform and not the one on the back." Merging the gifts and personalities of individuals into a cohesive team is no small challenge, but with God's help it can be done. Let me suggest nine steps for launching your team.

Step 1: Determine your ministry areas. You may want to categorize the entire ministry of your church into separate areas—for example, Christian education, building and maintenance, worship, fellowship, evangelism, and so forth. (See the seven Ministry Action Teams in chapter 6.) Ministry Action Teams may be appointed to supervise the ongoing ministries in those areas.

Teams for those ministry areas should be recruited and appointed on the basis of their skills and interests in those areas.

Step 2: Structure your team. How many members will be on the team? How long will the team serve? What is the main function of the team? These are among the questions that will be answered in a written job description that you will prepare for your team. Good delegation begins with good direction.

Chris Russell gives some excellent advice in his article "Effective Delegation" (*Today's Christian Preacher*, summer 1997):

Remember that it's best to delegate responsibilities rather than specific tasks. That way, you can provide general directions without having to keep assigning new tasks. Be sure the person has the authority to carry out the delegated responsibility. He or she must have the power to make decisions within the parameters you establish. Realize that it's not bad for lay people to make mistakes. As long as it's not the same mistake over and over, it shows that they're learning, growing, and trying new things.

Step 3: Evaluate the skills and personalities of potential team members. As has been said, each team member is unique. Ability levels will differ. Temperaments will differ. Personalities will differ. The skilled coach will see how those unique individuals may work together as a team. As a rule, however, potential teammates should have at least some degree of compatibility.

Of course, the first ingredient in structuring a team is prayer. God's Word promises, *If any of you lacks wisdom, let him ask of God, who gives to all liberally and without reproach, and it will be given to him* (James 1:5). Since He created them, God knows our potential team members far better than we ever will. He knows exactly which person belongs on your team.

Step 4: Choose your leaders. Red Auerbach, the great Boston Celtics coach, once remarked, "How you select people is more important than how you manage them once they are on the job." According to Bobb Biehl, "Having the right players determines 60 to 80 percent of the success of any organization." And having the right leaders is just as important! Choosing solid team leaders is one of the most crucial steps in creating exceptional Ministry Action Teams. One of the characteristics of an effective coach is the ability to spot good players. Paul modeled this trait in the case of Timothy:

> Then he [Paul] came to Derbe and Lystra. And behold, a certain disciple was there, named Timothy, the

son of a certain Jewish woman who believed, but his father was Greek. He was well spoken of by the brethren who were at Lystra and Iconium. Paul wanted to have him go on with him *(Acts 16:1-3).*

It is wonderful to be a naturally good trainer and to have a knack for picking potential leaders. But Jesus took it a step further. Before He engaged in training, He first spent all night in prayer, making sure He was picking just the right leaders: *Now it came to pass in those days that He went out to the mountain to pray, and continued all night in prayer to God. And when it was day, He called His disciples to Him; and from them He chose twelve whom He also named apostles* (Luke 6:12-13).

The 12 men Jesus chose for His team seemed destined for calamity, but He saw their potential. Although it appeared highly unlikely those 12 diverse men would be able to work together as a harmonious team, by Acts 2:1, *They were all with one accord in one place.* Jesus had molded them into a functional team. (But remember that they had their failures along the way—even to the point of deserting Jesus during the crucifixion experience. Don't despair when you see failure!)

Don Cousins shares four important steps to use in selecting the right players to lead the teams:

Strength of character. Nothing is more important! This involves traits such as discipline, honesty, teachability, humility, trustworthiness, and dependability.

Spiritual authenticity. Does the person have a heart that is fully the Lord's? Does he or she have a vital devotional life and share their faith with others? *For the eyes of the LORD run to and fro throughout the whole earth, to show Himself strong on behalf of those whose heart is loyal to Him* (2 Chron. 16:9).

Ministry fit. What people *do* ought to reflect who

they *are*—their spiritual gifts, temperament, passion, personality, and background.

Team fit. Team members who like each other and benefit from being around each other will work well together and bear much fruit.

In *Developing the Leaders Around You*, John Maxwell says that when he chooses leaders, he looks for people who:

- *Know his heart*, which takes time.
- *Are loyal to him*, for they are an extension of him and of his work.
- *Are trustworthy*, not abusing authority, power, or confidences.
- *Are discerning*, for they make decisions for him.
- *Have a servant's heart*, for they will carry a heavy load.
- *Are good thinkers*, for two heads are better than one.
- *Are able to follow through*, taking authority and carrying out the vision.
- *Have a great heart for God*, for that is the driving force in Maxwell's own life (Maxwell 1995, 9).

Step 5: Form the Team. Church researcher George Barna reports that "one out of every four adults (24 percent)" volunteer their free time to participate in the life of the church. Mobilizing this great volunteer army in skilled teams is key to the success of the local church.

There are some important procedures that should be considered when forming your teams:

- *Give everyone a chance.*
- *Make clear ministry assignments.*
- *Form ministry objectives that can be measured.*
- *Delegate with permission to fail.*
- *Demand accountability at every level of ministry.*
- *Evaluate and refine frequently. (Ministry plans should be tested against the overall vision plan of the church.)*

- *Be ready to make adjustments.*
- *Determine to persevere.*

On September 8, 1998, Mark McGwire broke the single-season home-run record (61) that was set by Roger Maris exactly two years, to the day, before McGwire was born. In the 144th game of the St. Louis Cardinals' 1998 season, the burly first baseman hit his shortest homerun of the season (342 feet) over the left-field fence and secured his place in baseball history. It was one of the biggest accomplishments to ever occur on a baseball diamond, but ironically, it was an event that nearly didn't occur.

After a frustrating season in 1991, when he hit only .201 and was hampered by foot and back injuries, McGwire seriously considered retiring. He classified himself as an emotional wreck and thought about giving up.

Before quitting, though, he remembered his dad's life-long battle with polio. John McGwire contracted polio at age 7 and walked with a cane because one leg was shorter than the other. Nonetheless, McGwire's father fought through his disability to become a successful dentist, an avid golfer, and a cyclist at 61 years of age. McGwire decided he couldn't quit even if the future didn't look very bright in baseball.

For the next four years he sought therapy to deal with his depression and persevered with his career even though he missed virtually all of the 1993 and 1994 seasons because of injuries. Then it happened. Seven years after thinking it was time to retire, Mark McGwire became the new Sultan of Swat. Incidentally, McGwire went to Southern Cal on a scholarship to pitch. It wasn't until his sophomore year that he made the transformation from a flame-throwing pitcher to a ball-crunching slugger. (Adapted from *Houston Chronicle*, September 9, 1998, sec. B, p. 5.)

Of course McGwire went on to establish the all-time home-run record with 70 round-trippers in 1998. Wouldn't it be great if the church world would capture that spirit of perseverance in the face of discouragement?

Step 6: Provide adequate training. Military leaders wouldn't think of sending their troops into battle without proper training. Neither should church leaders. In order to be prepared for their ministry assignments, laypersons need adequate training times. *What king, going to make war against another king, does not sit down first and consider whether he is able with ten thousand to meet him who comes against him with twenty thousand?* (Luke 14:31).

By virtue of its schedules, the local church has built-in training times. Sunday School, midweek services, preservice classes, and other opportunities can be turned into "basic training" sites for Ministry Action Team recruits. Resistance to breaking the traditional structures can be overcome by laying a thorough groundwork in teaching the entire congregation the importance of the teams and their biblical mandate.

The training times may include audiovisual presentations, class assignments, guest lectures, discussion times, informal refreshment times, and, of course, on-the-job practice. Every effort should be made to make the training sessions professional, yet personal.

The pastor-coach never knows what potential ministry standout may be in the class. The *Free Methodist* magazine gave these examples:

- A six-year-old lad came home with a note from his teacher in which it was suggested that he be taken out of school, as he was "too stupid to learn." That boy was Thomas A. Edison.
- Alfred Tennyson's grandfather gave him 10 shillings for writing his grandmother's eulogy. Handing it to the lad, the old man said: "There, that is the first money you ever earned by your poetry, and take my word for it, it will be the last."

- Benjamin Franklin's mother-in-law hesitated at letting her daughter marry a printer. There were already two printing offices in the United States, and she feared that the country might not be able to support a third.

Step 7: Give public recognition to the appointees.

The completion of the training sessions is a wonderful time to give a public recognition of the appointment, and the training efforts, of your Ministry Action Team. Everyone loves a celebration! A Sunday evening worship service, for instance, could include a presentation of the biblical mandate for ministry and a commissioning of the team. The service may also be a wonderful time to present the plan of salvation to guests of the team who have been invited to the commissioning service.

In his book *Sources of Strength*, former President Jimmy Carter recalled his walk down Pennsylvania Avenue with his family members following his inauguration. Carter's mother was instructed not to stop for reporter's questions, but she ignored the advice and responded to a reporter who commented, "Miss Lillian, aren't you proud of your son?"

The president said his mother replied, "Which one?"

Certainly your Ministry Action Team should understand that the "ground is level at the foot of the Cross"— that we have all been adopted into the same body. But a little recognition for the commitment and the efforts of team members will serve them well when the ministry load gets heavy and times of discouragement set in. They may look back to their commissioning service as a point of reference.

"Coach Paul" encouraged the church to give recognition to those who earn it, *Render therefore to all their due: taxes to whom taxes are due, customs to whom customs, fear to whom fear, honor to whom honor* (Rom. 13:7).

Step 8: Release them for ministry.
A Baptist church set its sights on a well-known down-and-outer in the com-

munity. They repeatedly invited the man to church but he refused their invitation, saying he didn't have good enough clothes to wear.

Finally, some of the members of the church decided to do something about his clothes excuse. They invited him to the neighborhood department store and bought him a beautiful new suit, shirt, tie, and shoes. "There!" The proud committee said, "We'll be looking for you this Sunday."

Sunday came, and there was no sign of the man with the new clothes. The preacher spotted him the next week and asked him why he didn't come to the church. "Well, the truth is, Reverend," the man answered, "I looked in the mirror and saw how good I looked and decided to go to First Presbyterian!"

Your Ministry Action Team may be well-dressed, well-trained, and well-recognized, but the time comes when they must be released for ministry in their appointed areas. The awful tendency in some churches is to spend too much time in training and not enough time in implementation.

The pastor-coach has already given the team "assignment with authority." Team members know they have the authority to minister within the parameters of their job description. Now it's time to send the team "out of the locker room" and onto the "playing field."

Pastor-coaches should resist the urge to micromanage. Ministry Action Team leaders should be given plenty of time and space for team leaders to do the job without feeling paranoid. They must learn to persevere in the "heat of the battle."

Og Mandino gives a great example of what can happen with perseverance.

One of Mandino's ten common causes of failure is "quitting too soon." Mandino tells the story of Raphael Solano and his companions who were looking for diamonds in a dry river bed. Discouraged, Solano claimed he had picked up about 999,999 rocks and was quitting. His companions said, "Pick up one more and make it a million." That "millionth" rock was "The Liberator," the largest and purest diamond ever found. Mandino writes, "I think he [Solano] must have known a happiness that went beyond the financial. He had set his course; the odds were against him; he had persevered; he had won. He had not only done what he had set out to do—which is a reward in itself—but he had done it in the face of failure and obscurity" *(Mandino 1982).*

Step 9: Conduct a debriefing session. After the Ministry Action Team completes its first assignment, it's time to bring them back together for a reporting time. This is a good place to discuss fears, failures, and triumphs in a nonthreatening environment.

It's also a good time for a pat on the back for a job "well tried." We all like to have our efforts appreciated. The encouragement you offer your team after its first assignment could well set the tone for all of its future endeavors.

A UPI press release told about President Gerald Ford's signing of a bill posthumously promoting George Washington to the rank of six-star general. Congress had awarded the rank for the man who would become the first president in a bill passed March 3, 1799, but then-President John Adams never got around to submitting Washington's name to the Senate for confirmation.

An effective pastor-coach or team leader is always "current" in the appreciation department!

Understanding Ministry Priorities

Review this search committee report:

In our search for a suitable pastor, the following scratch sheet was developed for your perusal. Of the candidates investigated by the committee, only one was found to have the necessary qualities. The list contains the names of the candidates and comments on each, should you be interested in investigating them further for future pastoral placements:

Noah: Has 120 years of preaching experience, but no converts.

Moses: Stutters, and his former congregation says he loses his temper over trivial things.

Abraham: Took off to Egypt during hard times. We heard that he got into trouble with the authorities and then tried to lie his way out.

David: Has an unacceptable moral character. He might have been considered for minister of music had he not fallen.

Solomon: Has a reputation for wisdom but fails to practice what he preaches.

Elijah: Proved to be inconsistent and is known to fold under pressure.

Hosea: His family life is in a shambles. Divorced and remarried to a prostitute.

Jeremiah: He is too emotional, alarmist; some say a real pain in the neck.

Amos: Comes from a farming background. Better off picking figs.

John: Says he is a Baptist but lacks tact and dresses like a hippie. Would not feel comfortable at a church potluck supper.

Peter: Has a bad temper and was heard to have even denied Christ publicly.

Paul: We found him to lack tact. He is too harsh, his appearance is contemptible, and he preaches far too long.

Timothy: He has potential but is much too young for the position.

Jesus: Tends to offend church members with his preaching, especially Bible scholars. He is also too controversial. He even offended the search committee with his pointed questions.

Judas: Seemed to be very practical, cooperative, good with money, cares for the poor, and dresses well. We all agreed that he is just the man we are looking for to fill the vacancy as our senior pastor.

Thank you for all you have done in assisting us with our pastoral search.

Sincerely,
The Pastoral Search Committee

While this search committee might rank as the toughest one ever, a pastor-coach who understands how to prioritize ministry in the local church will always rank high in the minds of its leaders.

Baseball legend Babe Ruth was asked how he always came through in the clutch—how he could step up to bat with the game on the line in the bottom of the ninth and hit the ball for a game-winning run.

Ruth answered in the simplest terms, "I just keep my eye on the ball."

Game-winning ministry focuses on priorities. And the first priority is to *seek first the kingdom of God and His righteousness* (Matt. 6:33).

The following vital areas deserve top priority for establishing Ministry Action Teams:

The context of ministry. The church family must understand why pastors do what they do.

Factors affecting ministry. All obstacles should be dealt with before leading ministry teams.

Planning for action. Ministry team members must have a voice in the development of key strategies.

Communication channels. Clear lines of information must be established.

Implementation stages and schedules. There should be specific target and scheduling deadlines for implementing team ministry.

Monitoring, review, and evaluation. An evaluation form should be created to monitor and review the progress of ministry teams.

The Leadership Legacy of John Wooden

Coach John Wooden's UCLA Bruins basketball team won an astonishing 88 games in a row, 36 consecutive playoff games, and 10 national championships. Citing teamwork as the key to victory, Wooden offers the following acrostic:

T ogether. We need to work together rather than as individuals.

E mpathy. We need empathy for all the team members.

A ssist. We need to assist in helping others.

M aturity. We need maturity in order to handle problems.

W illingness. We need to be willing to work together in harmony.

O rganization. We need proper organization in order to have a smooth operation.

R espect. We need respect for the coach and the other team members.

K indness. We need kindness for everyone we come into contact with.

Furthermore, John Wooden always stressed that "a team is a group of people working together for a common purpose." A group of people who do not know their common purpose is not a team—even though they may call themselves a team. A true team knows its calling. Just as

John Wooden's philosophy brought measurable results on the basketball court, so teamwork in the church will bring tangible results—growth upon growth.

Team-Building Tips

- Cross-train team leaders in a myriad of ministry skills.
- Create common expectations and understandings for all team members.
- Eliminate the duplication of ministry team endeavors.
- Use consensus decision making to establish team priorities.
- Celebrate the "special days" of your teammates.
- Evaluate team effectiveness.
- Hold team leaders accountable for decisions made.
- Ask for positive statements from negative teammates.
- Show respect for team members' families.
- Incorporate goals with appraisals.
- Give paid pastoral staff an annual salary increase based on team performance.
- Conduct a round-robin meeting to collect team ministry ideas.

Nonprofit organizations find it very hard to answer the question: "What, then, are the results in our institution?"

—Peter Drucker

5

Fine-Tuning Ministry Action Teams

We then, as workers together with Him
also plead with you not to receive
the grace of God in vain.

(2 Cor. 6:1)

MY (TOLER) COLLEGE BASKETBALL COACH, David Lattimer, was one of the most effective coaches I have ever played for. Coach Lattimer understood the strengths and weaknesses of every team member. He understood that my brother Terry was a great shooter and playmaker. He also knew that I was a baseball player wearing basketball clothes! Often, when he would send me into the game he would say, "Stan, remember two things: First, find the leading scorer and foul him till you foul out! Don't let him come into our house and act this way! And, second, whatever you do, don't shoot . . . uh . . . unless they give you a free throw. But be careful!" Frankly, at first I didn't understand why I wasn't allowed to shoot like my brother Terry. However, I ultimately realized that my role was very valuable to the team. I was never on the court long, but I was important because I *stopped* some great plays by the opposing team. At last I realized that I was an effective contributor to a winning team!

Celebrate Uniqueness

Legendary basketball player Bill Walton said, "In basketball, you may be the greatest player in the world and lose

every game, because a team will always beat an individual."
The church ministry team is God's instrument in meeting
the needs of people in your community, as well as in your
church. Your responsibility as pastor-coach is to encourage
laypersons to exercise the spiritual gifts God has given them
in a team effort to meet those needs.

Coach Lattimer obviously recognized my limited abilities and found the best "spot" for me on the team. Likewise,
if church teams are to be successful, the pastor-coach must
encourage the team to be enthusiastic about their unique
talents and their specialized areas of ministry.

Define Success in Practical Terms

Success is being where God places you, doing what God wants you to do, with the gifts He has given you.

—Larry Gilbert

It is not what laypersons are that holds them back, but what they think they aren't.
Many laypersons live way below their poten-
tial. Others are living up to their potential, but
have such low self-esteem that they don't acknowledge it. They are much more successful
than they think they are.

The task of the pastor-coach is to develop the potential of ministry team members by
making them aware of what true success really is. **"Successful" people are those who
have found God's will and are living in it
to the best of their abilities.** It has been
wisely said, "To know God's will is the greatest knowledge, to do God's will is the greatest
achievement."

When a pastor has a congregation who is
"doing God's will," it will be easier to recruit
Ministry Action Team members. Since the local church is
somewhat like a business corporation, Glenn M. Parker's
characteristics of a successful corporate team in his book

Team Players and Teamwork are highly relevant. They are:

Clear purpose. The vision, mission, goal, or task of the team has been defined and is now accepted by everyone. The mission statement has been followed up with an action plan.

Informality. The climate tends to be informal, comfortable, and relaxed, with no obvious tensions or signs of boredom.

Participation. There is much discussion and everyone is encouraged to be involved.

Listening. The members use effective listening techniques such as questioning, paraphrasing, and summarizing to get our ideas.

Civilized disagreement. There is disagreement, but the team is comfortable with it and shows no signs of avoiding, smoothing over, or suppressing conflict.

Consensus decisions. For important decisions, the goal is substantial, but not necessarily unanimous, agreement. This is based on an open discussion of everyone's ideas, and avoids formal voting or easy compromise.

Open communication. Team members feel free to express their feelings on the tasks as well as on the group's operation. There are few hidden agendas. Communication takes place both inside and outside meetings.

Clear roles and work assignments. There are clear expectations about the roles played by each team member. When action is taken, clear assignments are made, accepted, and carried out. Work is fairly distributed among team members.

Shared leadership. While the team has a formal leader, leadership functions shift from time to time depending upon the circumstances, the needs of the group, and the skills of the members. The formal leader models the appropriate behavior and helps establish positive norms.

External relations. The team spends time developing key outside relationships, mobilizing resources, and building credibility with important players in other parts of the organization.

Style diversity. The team has a broad spectrum of team-player types.

Self-assessment. Periodically, the team stops to examine how well it is functioning and what may be interfering with its effectiveness (Parker 1996, 81).

Trying to reverse the American buyer's trend toward purchasing imports, the Ford Motor Company made a bold move. A mid-sized car was designed and manufactured in a brand-new way. Traditionally, Ford designers made sketches and passed them on to manufacturing departments. For years designers etched out sketches, which were passed on to manufacturing departments. Sales received the finished product and had to figure out a way to sell it.

This time, a team was put together to handle the project from ground zero. Department heads were assembled and asked to make a wish list for an ideal car. From that point on, the manufacturing team worked to carry out the wishes of the vision-casting team. The result was one of the best-selling Ford products ever. More than 1 million units of the award-winning Taurus were sold in the first four years.

Working alone, those individual "experts" could not succeed. But, working as a team, those same gifted individuals wonderfully accomplished their goal. Why? In Bill Walton's words, "Because a team will always beat an individual."

Look for the Key Ingredients

Bottom Line magazine (Vol. 1, No. 3) lists key ingredients that all successful teams have in common:

The leader instills a shared sense of purpose. Ray Stato, chairman of Analog Devices Line, says, "The leader must create a sense of purpose, clarity of vision, and a conviction that the individuals of the team are world-class." Synergy is created when each team member shares the team's vision.

All goals become "team" goals. Unless the "whole team" wins, no one wins! Individual accomplishments are fine for the record books, but they're really an afterthought. The Boston Celtics won 16 NBA championships and never once had the league-leading scorer on their team. Good leaders speak in the first-person plural: "We need . . ." "Our deadline . . ." "The job before us . . ."

Individuality is celebrated. Teamwork doesn't discount individuality. Everyone has a unique personality, differing skills, and definitive hopes and fears. Olympian Mary Lou Retton once said, "A talented leader will remember those differences, appreciate them and use them to the advantage of the team."

Personal as well as corporate responsibility is shared. Projects belong to the team. Solutions may bubble up from the group, and that participation should be welcomed. But dictated or imposed decisions shouldn't come from the top. The team must solve the problem.

Sharing glory is accompanied by acceptance of blame. When the team does well, the benefits should be around. Share the glory, whether by a public pat on the back, a bonus, or a write-up in the church newsletter. Whatever form recognition takes, *every* team member should get a generous share of it. Al Abrour, former coach of the New York Islanders, used to say about his coaching style, "I praise in public, criticize in private."

Confidence-building is a continuous endeavor. A great leader believes firmly in the team. When a leader is always communicating positive confidence toward the team, a feeling develops among the teammates that they don't want to disappoint the leader or the group.

A Game Plan for Success
Develop a formula for winning
Position people for success
Focus on victory
Adjust today so you can win tomorrow

Solve Problems "Together"

One of the most important functions of highly effective teams is to find direction and solve problems—together. Teams can best find answers to problems by using a simple, eight-step process:

1. Discuss the history of the situation.
2. Establish a plan of action.
3. Determine potential pitfalls.
4. Dialogue about possible methods.
5. Ask: "What will be the most effective path?"
6. Share information with the team.
7. Get started immediately!
8. Monitor/review the results.

In *Team Building: An Exercise in Leadership*, Robert B. Maddux urges that problem-solving techniques be taught at every level of the organization. He recommends the following process:

The average pastor spends over ten hours a week going to meetings. The average congregation spends ninety people-hours considering whether or not to start a new ministry, only to say no to most of them.

—William Easum

State what appears to be the problem. The "real problem" may not surface until facts have been gathered and analyzed. Therefore, start with a supposition that can later be confirmed or corrected.

Gather facts, feelings, and opinions. *What* happened? *Where*, *when*, and *how* did it occur? What is the "real" size, scope, and severity of the problem? Who is affected by it? Is it likely to happen again? Does it really need to be corrected? Time and expense may require problem-solvers to think through the actual need and assign priorities to the more critical elements.

Restate the problem. Reiterating the facts may provide supporting data. The actual problem may or may not be the same as the one stated in *Step 1*.

Identify alternative solutions. Generate ideas. Do not eliminate any possible solutions until several have been discussed.

Evaluate alternatives. Which will provide the *optimum* solution? What are the risks? Are the costs in keeping with the benefits? Will the solution create new problems?

Implement the decision. Who must be involved? To what extent? How, when, and where? Who will the decision impact? What might go wrong? How will results be reported and verified?

Evaluate the results. Test the solution against the desired results. Modify the solution if better results are needed (Maddux 1992, 19).

Model the Best of the Best: "AMEs" and "RSAs"

A good example of highly effective Ministry Action Teams comes from one of Delaware's fastest-growing churches, Glasgow Reformed Presbyterian Church. They are using evangelism teams based in house churches as their primary tool for reaching the lost. In order to do this, they have developed two specific teams, called AMEs and RSAs:

"AMEs" are Acquaintance-Making Events. An AME is an event for the purpose of introducing unsaved and unchurched friends to other church members. These events usually take place in larger groups (more than eight), and never one-on-one. They are planned ahead of time and organized. AMEs are social gatherings: picnics, cookouts, parties, hospitality events, afternoon teas. They usually take place outside the church. Their purpose is simple: to help develop a three-way relationship or friendship bridge among the church member, his or her invited unsaved and unchurched friend, and the regular members of the group. When planning AMEs, laypersons must remember four basic rules:

- Be sure to invite unsaved and unchurched friends every time the group has a social function.
- Be careful about being too pushy.
- Be sure to mingle, and do not ignore the newcomers.
- Be patient.

> *Trusting relationships are the key to reaching people for Christ and bonding them to His church.*
>
> —Larry Gilbert

"RSAs" are Relationship-Strengthening Activities. RSAs are activities for the purpose of developing, cultivating, strengthening, and building trusting relationships between unchurched friends and other church members. These activities usually take place in smaller groups (four or less), or even one-on-one. RSAs are more informal than AMEs in the sense that they are less planned, more spontaneous, and may include such activities as shopping trips, dining out, or watching the game on television. When involved in RSAs, laypersons must remember to: Not be on the edge of their seats all evening, looking for the perfect time to twist the conversation into a presentation of the gospel. Instead, they should **allow God to open the opportunity at the natural time. Be a good witness at all times, in entertainment, conduct, and dress. Don't condemn or belittle the friends' lifestyles.**

This approach keeps individual Christians from having to "go it alone" in their efforts to fulfill the Great Commission. The group works together as an evangelism *team* to support each other, pray for their lost friends, and create the environment of friendship needed to introduce newcomers to Christ and His church. *Acquaintance-Making Events* and *Relationship-Strengthening Events* are great ways for bringing the *seeker* and the *nonseeker* into the church's sphere of influence.

> *It is important to recognize that not every unsaved or unchurched person is truly a seeker. Seeker-oriented methodology generally won't work for reaching, or even influencing, nonseekers in today's culture.*
> —Larry Gilbert.

Learn from the America's Cup Team

The America's Cup yachting challenge pits the world's top sailors against the forces of nature, exacting from them their greatest efforts as they represent their various countries. Without a crew, the finest yacht-building efforts would be to no avail. The ship simply can't sail by itself! And, without a skipper the crew would lack the direction necessary to carry out their task.

Such is the case with the pastor-coach and team ministry. As with the AME and RSA outreach ministries mentioned, pastors need laypersons to bring their friends to church to *hear* the sermons they've prepared. Similarly, laypersons need pastors to *preach those sermons* to the friends they've brought to church. Pastors and laypersons (the skipper and the crew) need to work together. Good coordinated teamwork is the key to effective church ministry.

As a yachting captain encourages the crew to their ultimate performance, so pastor-coaches must take the initiative to mold their congregation into an excellent ministry team. In turn, the pastor-coach must be willing to accept **God's molding** to best meet the needs of the congregation.

Troubleshooting

Sir Michael Costa, the celebrated conductor, was holding a rehearsal. As the mighty chorus rang out, accompanied by scores of instruments, the piccolo player thought he could quit playing without being missed since there was so much music being played. Suddenly the great leader stopped and cried out: "Where is the piccolo?" The sound of that one small instrument was necessary for the full harmony of the musical score, and the skilled conductor's ear had missed it when it did not play. So it is with your congregation. Every part (including the conductor—the pastor) must be played, and played in tune, or the whole congregation will suffer.

But what if a part is played out of tune or not played at all because of dissension? All your hard work as a pastor-coach could be in jeopardy. Sometimes a shift to team building can be going amazingly smooth only to be destroyed by internal problems. Wise leaders will be on the alert to these barriers of team ministry success. Preventive medicine is always the best policy. (Effective ministry team leaders never wait until things are at a critical impasse before they take action.)

The following will point out signs of trouble and offer remedies, so that obstacles to success can be overcome before they harm your church's ministry.

Watch for Danger Signs

A good team leader must be able to recognize symptoms of trouble within the group. Tim Rudlaff offers these 10 signs that your team has underlying difficulties that need to be addressed:

1. ***Meetings are formal and tense.*** Be concerned if team members are not seemingly relaxed during meeting times. Team players should be creative and dynamic when they are together. ***Remedy:*** Open all meetings with prayer, icebreakers, and a humorous story.

2. ***Teammates participate but don't achieve.*** When team members start enjoying social interaction but fail to get much accomplished, it is a warning sign. ***Remedy:*** Appoint a team leader who is a "doer."

3. ***Teammates talk but don't communicate.*** Some people don't want to listen—they only want to talk. Team communications should be an interactive give-and-take. ***Remedy:*** Ask the team to summarize what has been said. Appoint a team "scribe" to write down vital information that has been shared.

4. ***Disputes are resolved in private after team meetings.*** Healthy teams have open discussions about their differences. Private discussions of team matters quickly build distrust. ***Remedy:*** Feedback should be shared only when the entire team is present.

5. ***The team leader is making most of the decisions.*** This can happen if the leader is too aggressive or the team members are too quiet. Every member needs to contribute —that's why it's called a team. ***Remedy:*** Ask the team leader to keep a list of those involved in the process and share it with the senior pastor on a monthly basis.

6. ***Team members don't trust each other.*** When a team is starting, this can be expected. However, lack of trust is a serious problem. ***Remedy:*** Appoint only trustworthy leaders.

7. ***There is confusion about ministry roles.*** Whenever there are misunderstandings or conflicts about assignments, things need to be clarified quickly. **Remedy**: Distribute copies of all ministry job descriptions.

8. *Team members publicly criticize or embarrass others.* If legitimate feedback or criticism needs to be discussed, it must be done in private—never in front of other team members. ***Remedy:*** Confront the team leaders with care and concern. Emphasize the importance of esteeming the ministry team members.

9. *Things are promised that are not delivered.* This generally indicates mistrust or a spirit of carelessness toward the team, and it wears down morale. ***Remedy:*** Establish accountability lines and ask for periodic updates.

10. *Confidences are broken.* This causes team members to lose respect for one another. They will become reluctant to talk for fear of what their teammates will do with the information. ***Remedy:*** Find a new team leader quickly!

—Adapted from *CopyFast Print Shop Newsletter* (McWilliams, ed. 1999).

> In Him you also trusted, after you heard the word of truth, the gospel of your salvation; in whom also, having believed, you were sealed with the Holy Spirit of promise, who is the guarantee of our inheritance until the redemption of the purchased possession, to the praise of His glory. Therefore I also, after I heard of your faith in the Lord Jesus and your love for all the saints, do not cease to give thanks for you, making mention of you in my prayers; that the God of our Lord Jesus Christ, the Father of glory, may give to you the spirit of wisdom and revelation in the knowledge of Him *(Eph. 1:13-17).*

Avoid "Gift Imposing"

"Gift imposing" is the act of forcing your own spiritual gift upon another person and attempting to compel that person to perform it as though it were his or her gift. For example, "Gift imposers" want the whole body to be an "eye"—or whatever "member" *they* may be. Such individuals fail to recognize the diversity of the Body of Christ, and as a result, force other Christians to function in capacities for which God has not gifted them.

Gift imposers give the impression that the area of ministry for which God has gifted and burdened them is *superior* to all others. In fact, some not only subtly give that impression but also openly declare that *their gifts* are the only ones that count. They may even determine that there is only *one gift*—and that gift belongs to them! Gift imposers distribute much frustration, discouragement, and false guilt among others on the ministry team.

Gift imposers also use guilt trips to force their gifts on others. They try to make others feel that they are not right with God unless they are involved with the same ministry as they are. For example, some people have the gift of evangelism. They are motivated and consumed with personally leading people to Christ. They witness with tracts and confront people on the street, in doctors' offices, on the bus—anywhere and anytime they can. When they find fellow Christians with another gift—the gift of serving or the gift of mercy, for instance—and see those people are not out on the streets witnessing like them, the "evangelist" accuses them of not being "burdened for souls."

In reality, that evangelist's assessment may be far from the truth. Someone with the gift of mercy may actually have been responsible for many coming to Christ. And the server may have opened doors the evangelist could only have wished to open. No believer who uses his or her gift properly should feel guilty for not having the same gift as someone else.

Gift imposers work in two basic ways: first, they try to convince others of their great "burden"; second, they try to convince others by repeating their message—they become "one-string banjos," restating the same theme week in and week out. This drives many potential workers away and makes those workers who stay think the gift imposer's gift or ministry is all there is.

Remedy: As a friend, speak with the person who is imposing his or her gift on others. The following advice is good for both the gift imposer as well as the person who may feel imposed upon: "We all have heroes in the work of God, people we consider great and outstanding because of their positions and accomplishments. But God has called each individual to do something unique. The church needs the manifestation of **each** gift. You are accountable for the gift God has given you—not for God's calling on someone else's life." In order for the gift imposer to understand his or her "unique" place in ministry, the pastor-coach may want to help that individual understand several important principles of gift-use:

- Do what God has called you to do.
- Make your personal ministry a real matter of prayer, allowing God to reveal His place for you in ministry.
- Don't allow people to impose their gifts on you, and don't gravitate to, or colonize with, those who have the same gift as you.
- Don't be blind to others' gifts, but don't covet gifts God gave to someone else. He made no mistake when He gave your gift to you (see 1 Cor. 12:18).

It is easy to fall into Satan's traps. He specializes in causing people to go to *bad* extremes over *good* things. Much of the guilt associated with Christian ministry is not conviction from the Holy Spirit, but false guilt caused by not living up to the expectations of others.

Deal with "Control Issues"

As a church grows, the pastor's *hands-on ministry* must decrease and the congregation's *hands-on ministry* must increase. This will be especially difficult for pastors who need to "control." Top-down, oppressive, and dictatorial manage-ment is out in today's society. There is no room for a *boss-pastor*. A pastor's willingness to move to a team ministry is crucial to the effectiveness of a church's ministry!

Tim LaHaye's well-known basic personality traits will factor into whether or not a pastor has control issues. Ex-amine these traits and honestly evaluate yourself.

The phlegmatic finds it easy to allow others to lead. Because of this, the phlegmatic sometimes needs to take more control than he or she actually wants.

The melancholic easily gets lost in mundane details and might "muddy the water" for team leaders.

The sanguine just wants to have fun. Life is a party! They want everyone to be happy and have a tendency to be more interested in chatting and making friends than in actual leading.

The choleric has a tendency to be bossy and finds it hard to let go of the reins. For example, this person may be-come a *pastor-controller*—with the following characteristics:

The Pastor-Controller

1. Has a lone ranger mentality. "No one does it like me."
2. Limits decision making to a small inner circle.
3. Is ego-centered. "No one cares for people like I do." (I.e., making hospital calls. They get their strokes and affirmation from ministry, so it's hard for them to let go of these areas.)
4. Pushes personal agendas.
5. Has a watchdog mentality that results in critical and negative behavior. (In other words, watches for mis-takes rather than encouraging and serving as a re-source.)
6. Is inflexible with schedules, programs, innovations. "It's my way or the highway."

Remedy: The pastor-controller should focus on becoming a pastor-coach who:

1. Is willing to share in problem solving, vision casting, managing teams, and decision making.
2. Develops guidelines of how teams will function.
3. Values giftedness in team members.
4. Keeps agreements.
5. Communicates the mission.
6. Is flexible.
7. Listens and understands team dynamics.
8. Makes the ministry people oriented.
9. Uses the Word of God as a guide for ministry. (See Acts 6 as an example of giving up control and letting others serve.)
10. Helps Christians grow to maturity.

Sometimes the boss-pastor finds it difficult to release control because of an issue with trust—and trust is a very important factor in cultivating effective teams. *Remedy:* Charles Handy, in *The Hungry Spirit* (Broadway Books), lists several principles of trust that will assist the pastor-controller with implementing Ministry Action Teams as a pastor-coach:

Trust is not blind. To trust people we must know them. Take the time to develop relationships and bond with laypersons.

Trust requires constant learning. We must be open to new ideas for strengthening our teams. We should be discerning—knowing when to offer opinions and when not to.

Trust is tough. Gaining the trust of your congregation can take time and effort. Likewise, it takes time and effort to extend trust to individual laypersons. Pray that God will give you the strength to trust.

Beware of Ego Trips!

Ruth N. Koch and Kenneth C. Haugk, in their book *Speaking the Truth in Love* (St. Louis: Stephen Ministries, 1992), tell of an incident in the career of former Dallas Cowboy head coach Tom Landry. He was lecturing his players after a game about their various antics after each touchdown. One had danced, another had wiggled, and still another had spiked the ball.

Landry said with a stern voice, "Act like you've been in the end zone before!" The coach wanted his players to be seen as competent team members, not individual "hot shots."

Nothing will destroy ministry teamwork faster than selfishness among team members. Several years ago, composer-performer Lionel Richie wrote and produced the popular song "We Are the World." He invited the luminaries of the music industry to cooperate on the record in order to raise money for starving people. On the day of the recording, he posted a sign next to the studio entrance that said, "Check your ego at the door." Richie's message was clear: The success of the record depends on everyone working *together* for a common purpose instead of merely promoting themselves.

Likewise, ministry team leaders need to understand that the defining moments in their lives may well occur in the context of a *team* victory rather than an individual accomplishment. Pat Riley, coach of the Miami Heat basketball team, once said, "My driving belief is that great teamwork is the only way to reach our ultimate moments, to create the breakthroughs that define our career, to fulfill our lives with a sense of lasting significance."

Team-Building Tips
- Discover and develop the best talent you can.
- Give out rewards at the end of a team project.

- Lead by example!
- Emphasize the importance of disciplined work habits.
- Gain loyalty by making team members feel special.
- Mentor others and you will multiply team effectiveness.
- Select leaders based on their commitment to Jesus Christ.
- Deal with team disagreement with discretion.
- Train team members to discover their spiritual gifts and unique personality traits.
- Emphasize team relationships and de-emphasize rules.
- Model openness and caring.
- Recruit people for specific ministries.

6

Modeling Ministry: Team-Based Ministry Action Teams at Trinity Church of the Nazarene

And when they had prayed, the place where they were assembled together was shaken; and they were all filled with the Holy Spirit, and they spoke the word of God with boldness. Now the multitude of those who believed were of one heart and one soul; neither did anyone say that any of the things he possessed was his own, but they had all things in common. And with great power the apostles gave witness to the resurrection of the Lord Jesus. And great grace was upon them all. Nor was there anyone among them who lacked; for all who were possessors of lands or houses sold them, and brought the proceeds of the things that were sold.

(Acts 4:31-34)

TWO MEN WERE RIDING a bicycle built for two. Everything seemed to be going well until they started up a rather large hill, and then the struggle ensued. When they reached the top, the man on the first seat was gasping for breath. He looked back at his partner and said, "That hill took a lot out of me!" The man in the second seat said, "You're right, if I hadn't kept the brakes on all the way, we would have rolled back down the hill!"

This delightful story gives us an insight into the church's ministry. When it comes to change, for instance, some people feel they are just doing their duty when they try to put the brakes on every bit of upward progress that is proposed.

Lessons from My Home Church

My (Toler) home church in Columbus, Ohio, recently closed. Just 30 years ago that church thrived as one of the largest in the city. Their mistake? With community changes all around them, they put the brakes on change in their church.

I visited the church nine months before it closed the doors. (My parents stayed with the church until its final service.) While I was there, I made several observations. For example, they continued in the same nonessential traditions without giving thought to what the rest of the church world was doing. They opened Sunday School as they did in the '60s—singing the same birthday song, handing out the same pencils, and allowing "pencil recipients" to put pennies for missions in the same plastic birthday cake that was used when I was a teen. Nothing was innately wrong with any of their dated traditions—except that they were competing with the "church down the street" that had fine-tuned its ministry to specifically target contemporary needs.

My home church never changed its belief in the Word of God, the sacraments of the church, or the essentials of the faith. And they shouldn't have! Those fundamentals must be our anchor in time of change. But neither did that church change their *presentation* of those "anchor" fundamentals. Putting the brakes on change became its downfall.

> Most
> methods of
> evangelism
> that have
> worked in the
> past are not
> working
> today.
> —Alan Nelson

New Methods for a New Day

Robert Kriegel wrote a book in 1992 titled *If It Ain't Broke, Break It!* The target audience was corporate America. The book explored the concepts of working smarter, and the idea of unleashing creative thought in the workforce. Certainly the church can learn some things about cultural relevance from the marketplace. There are times when we need to break our nonessential tradition.

When I (Toler) was trained to witness

and evangelize we used the confrontational style. Today, people don't respond to that style as readily as they do to the relationship method. Ministering in the 21st century calls for building relationship bridges to win souls. Trusting relationships are the key to reaching people for Christ and bonding them to His church.

Research done by church-growth expert Win Arn shows that the more relationships an individual has within the church, the more apt that individual is to stay in the church. Conversely, the fewer relationships an individual has in the church, the less likely that individual will stay in the church. O. J. Bryson calls it "the rule of seven." When a church member has seven close friends in a church, he or she is unlikely to ever leave it. As Elmer Towns says, "Relationship is the glue that makes people stick to the church."

Other research shows that 86 percent of those who accept Christ and join a church do so because of the influence of a friend or a relative—an existing relationship. In essence,

It's our job as leaders to keep up with what works NOW! Methods change, but the message never changes!
—Stan Toler

Five specific characteristics denote whether something needs "breaking" in a church:

1. The church is focused on itself, rather than the needs of the world around it.
2. Perpetual conflict with church members standing opposite of one another.
3. The people have no vision spiritually and no vision for the future of the church.
4. Membership has plateaued or is declining.
5. Facilities are unkempt. (An easy problem to remedy!)

the more relationships nonseekers have with those who attend church, the greater the chance they will become receptive to the gospel. *Thus, if I want my unchurched friend to believe in Christ and to attend my church, I must get my friend to establish a trusting relationship with as many of my churched friends as possible.*

The Trinity Vision

When I (Toler) accepted the pastorate of Trinity Church of the Nazarene, I inherited a church with an excellent 63-year history, good pastors, and a track record of ministry success in the community.

I sought the Lord's guidance in building on that strength. Through research and counsel, I began to see the need for training leaders who would share the vision God had given me for the church. In the process, I discovered some workable ministry principles.

Preparation Is the Key to Growing the Church

Churches will not grow without preparing to grow. Churches don't "catch" growth like a cold, they make it a point to be farther ahead spiritually, financially, and numerically, than they were previously. Preparation is important in any field of endeavor. Malcolm Fleschner writes:

Preparation is part of the secret of the success of hockey superstar, Wayne Gretzky. Gretzky is far and away the greatest hockey player of all time. On March 23, 1994, Gretzky scored his 802nd career goal, breaking the only important scoring record that remained out of his grasp. In all, Gretzky now holds more than 60 game, season, playoff and career scoring records. In the 1980s, Gretzky won the National Hockey League's Most Valuable Player award, an unprecedented nine of ten possible times. No athlete in any other sport in history comes close to this kind of domination over the record books. Gordie Howe, who owned the old goal-scoring record, needed 26 years to put that many pucks in the net. Gretzky did it in 15.

But you wouldn't know it to look at him. He stands smaller than average for a hockey player—5'11"—and at 170 pounds weighs less than average too. He doesn't skate particularly fast or gracefully, his shot is not a real "burner" and on strength tests administered to each member of his team, Gretzky always placed dead last. So what makes the Great One so great?

Gretzky credits his father with dozens of essential lessons, from practicing his stick handling in the off-season with a tennis ball (Tennis balls are harder to control than pucks and teach you how to swat things out of the air) to attempting the unconventional.

"In practice," he says, "I try weird things like bouncing the puck off the side of the net to a teammate. I practiced it so much I can do it now in any direction. It's the same with the sideboards. People say there's only six men on the ice, but really, if you use the angle of deflection off the board, there's seven. If you count the net, that's eight. From the opening face-off, I always figure we have 'em, eight-on-six." Gretzky is the best prepared member of his team *(Fleschner 1994, 72)*.

11 Steps for Growth

During my first year as pastor of Trinity we took some definite, preplanned steps toward casting a new vision. The following 11 steps detail what our "ministry vision team" did to move the church forward into 21st century.

1. *Every Sunday evening for four weeks we conducted "church town meetings" in lieu of our Sunday evening service.* Eleven team leaders were trained in small-group assessment and evaluation methods, asked to read Rick

Warren's *Purpose-Driven Church*, and given specific discussion quotas for each meeting. Additionally, the team leaders met each Wednesday evening and discussed what went on in their small-group meetings. Based on congregational feedback, we were prepared to move forward in ministry.

2. *The Ministry Vision Team refined the mission statement of the church.* Concern was given to include wording that reflected the Great Commission and the Great Commandment. Here is what we came up with:

The Mission of Trinity Church

To know Christ and make Him known to others. As we come to know Him, we are changed to be more like Him.

---

3. *A vision plan was written to reflect our plans to implement the "seven ships" of Trinity.*

The Vision of
Trinity Church of the Nazarene
Serving in the 21st Century

OUR VISION	OUR FOCUS
S eeking God	**Worship**
E xtending Grace	**Friendship**
R eceiving Direction	**Discipleship**
V iewing the Future	**Leadership**
I nvolving People	**Partnership**
N urturing Life	**Fellowship**
G iving Generously	**Stewardship**

4. *We then designed a values statement to hold us steady in a time of change.*

Our Seven Core Values

1.	We value the souls of the lost.	Luke 19:10
2.	We value personal integrity.	Prov. 10:9
3.	We value corporate worship.	Heb. 10:25
4.	We value the Word of God.	Deut. 6:6-9
5.	We value the gifts of God's people.	Eph. 4:11-13
6.	We value wholesome fellowship.	1 John 1:7
7.	We value God's family.	Psalm 133:1

---

5. The "committee" system was changed to "Ministry Action Teams." Since every great team has a clear job description for its team members, as part of my organizational process at Trinity, I met with every existing committee and chairperson and sought understanding as to their role in the church. With the help of Pastor Jeffrey Johnson, I then attempted to bring role definition and team understanding into sharp focus. The newly organized teams were empowered to act and to spend funds according to a present budget. They were released to do ministry based on our new vision plan.

6. A Welcome Center was designed and built to meet the needs of our guests. Information packets were designed to share with our special visitors each Sunday.

7. A "Pastor's Welcome Class" was started for the purpose of sharing our vision for reaching our community for Christ. We determined that our community needed to know not only that Trinity Church of the Nazarene was there but also *why* it was there.

8. Our Friendship Ministry Team began a "Pastor's Brunch" that followed the Sunday worship service every 60 days. All guests who attended during the previous two months were invited to have lunch with the pastoral staff and key lay leaders.

9. *The Sunday School underwent some innovative changes.* A "Generation Excellence Class" was added, as were additional special electives classes.

10. *Cultural and leadership training opportunities were offered.* These were in the form of Lay Institute To Equip (LITE) and Strategic Advanced Leadership Training (SALT). These training opportunities began to move us toward becoming a learning organization.

11. *The traditional worship service received a "face-lift."* The worship service included the blending of hymns and praise choruses into our worship.

Four Key Questions

During these important steps, we kept four key questions before the leaders of the ministry teams:

- Who are we and what are our beliefs and values?
- What are our demographic possibilities for outreach?
- If we believe we are living in the end times, are we willing to work like it?
- Does this church belong to God, or to an internal controlling faction?

The Vision-Planning Team

Last, we began redefining the role of the church board. My first goal was to move us from dealing with "nickel and dime" issues to becoming a vision-planning team. The following statements reveal that new direction at Trinity:

THE MINISTRY VISION TEAM

PURPOSE OF THE MINISTRY VISION TEAM:

It is the purpose of this team to give direction to the life and ministry of this church toward the accomplishment of the church's mission as stated by Christ. Accomplishing this purpose will involve:

Developing and maintaining a strong, well-balanced, and inspirational church program that ministers to the needs of every age-group so that all may grow and mature in discipleship.

Developing and maintaining a definite program that involves our people in the outreach of the church. Doing so will require that we provide training, assistance, and direction as necessary for maximum effectiveness.

Obtaining and maintaining facilities that are functional in nature, adequate in size, and equipped with sufficient equipment.

Developing and maintaining a program of financial support that is strong enough to underwrite these programs and facilities.

ORGANIZATION OF THE MINISTRY VISION TEAM:

To assure that positive attention is given to each of these areas, this team shall be organized as follows:

A total of 16 team (church board) members and 3 ex officio members.

The 3 ex officio members are missions teamleader, youth team leader, and the Sunday School superintendent.

The team will elect corporate officers within the team by a ballot vote. These elected officers will serve as secretary and treasurer.

The board members will be appointed to serve in one of seven ministry teams. The seven Ministry Action Teams are:

- Fellowship
- Stewardship
- Worship
- Friendship
- Partnership
- Leadership
- Discipleship

The 3 auxiliary officers and departments (youth, missions and Sunday School) will be structured according to church manual requirements.

RESPONSIBILITIES OF THE MINISTRY VISION TEAM:

Team members are limited to a maximum of three consecutive one-year terms of service.

Team members must rotate off the Ministry Vision Team for one year. It is expected that individuals leaving the team will be involved in subcommittee work.

The three-year tenure also includes the ex officio members (youth team leader, missions team leader, and Sunday School superintendent).

The Ministry Vision Team will meet monthly to hear reports, review of minutes, conduct an annual audit, study statistics, review plans and take appropriate action for the general operation of the church. Attendance at each monthly meeting is expected.

"Resigning" as the Chairman of the Board

One assignment that I disliked the most in church work was being the "chairman of the church board." I have never enjoyed chairing meetings. Frankly, I talk too much to be a chairman! Further, I tend to be thin-skinned when church board members are critical about a specific topic.

I finally resolved the matter. I "resigned" as chairman of the board and appointed a qualified layperson in my place. I came to the realization that people were not criticizing me in the board meetings—they were merely trying to deal with areas of church ministry that needed help. They were the ones who cared enough to point out the problems! I then decided that a layperson chairing the meetings could "take the heat" better than I. What a discovery! To my surprise, I found that most board members were "kinder and gentler" to their peers.

With the new understanding that I didn't have to chair all the meetings nor even be present for all the meetings (I do make most of the board meetings), I felt a great sense of release to do ministry. More than ever before, I was able to fulfill my *best* gifts!

I hasten to point out that I still have an important role in the church board meeting, which we now call the Ministry Vision Team meeting. My role is to cast the vision! Therefore, I try never to get caught up in the mundane matters, for I am there to lead the church board to a new level of ministry.

I also point out that the governmental structures for local churches in some denominations might prohibit pastors from letting a layperson chair the church board meeting. Pastors are well advised to seek the counsel of their supervisors before making a change in their church board structure.

Ministry Vision Team Leaders

Now that I have mentioned the use of a board president, I would like to describe the role of this **Ministry Vision Team** leader. The following job description has been written for this important team leader at Trinity:

MINISTRY VISION TEAM PRESIDENT

The Ministry Vision Team president will:

- Lead Ministry Vision Team for a one-year term of service.
- Guide the agenda for each Ministry Vision Team meeting.
- Serve as assistant to the pastor on the Executive Ministry Team.
- Prepare the agenda for the Ministry Vision Team meeting as a result of the Executive Ministry Team meeting, with the approval of the senior pastor and

with consultation for additional action items. Submit the agenda to the church office for typing.

- Assist the senior pastor in watch care of the staff and their families.
- Spend quality time in encouragement of the team leaders and their various committees.
- Sign documents, checks, and other church papers as appropriate.
- Call Ministry Vision Team meetings with the approval of the senior pastor, and/or the district superintendent in the absence of the senior pastor. No Ministry Vision Team meeting will be called without such approval.
- Chair any specially called corporate officer meetings. Meetings are to be called with the approval of the senior pastor and whenever possible, at a time when the senior pastor can attend. The senior pastor is ex officio chairperson of all boards and committees of the local church.
- Assist the pastor with the affairs and activities of the church, with love and loyalty for all.

Ministry Action Team Leaders

After establishing a team leader for the church board, the next important issue was the employment of **Ministry Action Team** leaders. These individuals were appointed by the senior pastor (and still are) to head up the "seven ships" that were mentioned earlier. After many meetings in the study committees at Trinity, we were able to develop the following job description for our team leaders:

- Ministry Action Team leaders will be appointed by the pastor. This appointment will be for a one-year term of service.
- Ministry Action Team leaders can be appointed for more than one year, but they cannot lead the same

team for two consecutive years. (This does not include the Stewardship Ministry Action Team.)

- Each team leader will make a monthly report to the Executive Ministry Team and to the Ministry Vision Team.
- Each team leader is responsible for submitting to the Executive Ministry Team any expenditure that needs additional approval.
- Monthly committee information submitted by the team leaders will form the completed agenda for the next Ministry Vision Team meeting.
- Team leaders should meet monthly with their teammates. They should never conduct a meaningless meeting—meetings should be canceled if there is no reason for them.

Ministry Action Team Guidelines

Every leader needs a team. The following clarify the expectations I established for the Ministry Action Teams:

- Each team will consist of a leader and at least two members.
- Each team is expected to meet once a month. The leader is responsible for communicating the time, date and place of each meeting.
- Each team will have financial guidelines (recommended by the Stewardship Ministry Action Team and ratified by the Ministry Vision Team) that entitles each team to make financial decisions independent of Ministry Vision Team approval.
- Each team will have a financial ceiling cap that will require certain expenditures to be approved by the Executive Ministry Team.
- Each team is responsible to involve nonboard members and church attendees to serve on ministry teams.

- The auxiliary committees (youth, missions, and Sunday School) are to be structured according to manual requirements. Each of these auxiliary presidents and superintendents will be assigned a Ministry Action Team leader to assist them in ministry when needed.

The goal is involvement. Measure the success of events by the number of people you involve in the process.

Since I have been discussing ministry in general terms, the following example of our Partnership Ministry Action Team may provide additional insight and offer a guideline for the teams you choose to develop:

Partnership Ministry Team

Purpose of the Team:

- To direct the maintenance, improvement, and development of all church properties and equipment to assure adequate and functional facilities to meet the needs of the total program and growth of the local church under the Partnership Ministry Action Team.

Responsibilities of the Team:

- To provide for maintenance and improvements of all church-owned buildings, keeping them in attractive and functional condition at all times.
- To provide for maintenance and improvement of all grounds, grass, and shrubbery; to supervise landscape improvements; and to secure snow/ice removal when necessary.
- To provide for care and maintenance of all church-owned equipment and vehicles and to keep a current inventory of same.
- To recommend, for Ministry Vision Team approval, policy for the use of all facilities and equipment and to

provide for periodic review of existing policy to assure appropriate updating or changing.

- To supervise the work of all custodial personnel.
- To provide for and maintain the security of the church building.
- To anticipate need for additional equipment and to recommend, for Monthly Vision Team approval, the acquisition of additional equipment when needed.
- To provide for adequate insurance coverage for the church.
- To prepare an asking budget and to present same to the Executive Ministry Team in preparation of the annual church budget.

GUIDING QUESTION:

How can we equip and maintain our total facilities to provide the best possible environment for our local ministries?

MINISTRY TEAM LEADER
JOB DESCRIPTION

Purpose:

To oversee the involvement of many people in the maintenance, improvement, and development of all church properties and equipment to assure adequate functional facilities to meet the needs of the total program and growth of Trinity Church of the Nazarene.

Function:

To encourage, recruit, and appoint the necessary personnel to provide for the best possible environment for the ministries of Trinity Church of the Nazarene.

Responsibilities:

- Conduct monthly Buildings and Properties Ministry Team

meetings and report to the Ministry Vision Team (church board)

- Appoint leaders for these ministry areas:
  - Maintenance
  - Security
  - Equipment
  - Motor Vehicles
  - Facilities Insurance/Policy/Custodial Supervision
  - Property Improvements
  - Office Equipment
  - Lay Ministry Fair
- Oversee the financial planning and stewardship in these areas
- Coordinate planning in these areas with pastoral staff
- Meet monthly with Executive Ministry Team

Where Does the Pastoral Staff Fit In?

So where does the paid staff fit into all of this? The answer is simple: They are part of the church ministry team and must learn to work with Ministry Action Team leaders. There's no room for lone ranger types on the team. Every staff member matches up with a team leader and is asked to resource and encourage the lay ministers with whom they work. The following job description for the pastoral team has provided guidance for the paid leadership team at Trinity.

Pastoral Team Guidelines

- The senior pastor and staff will meet weekly in a regular session to deal with spiritual and administrative matters of the church.
- The staff will work with the appropriate Ministry Action Team leaders to facilitate their individual ministries.
- The Executive Ministry Team and Ministry Action Teams are to work with the staff to facilitate the ministries of the staff as well.

- The staff will make any financial request that needs additional approval to their Ministry Action Team leader.
- The team leader is responsible for taking this matter to the appropriate team, or the Executive Ministry Team, if needed.
- The pastor maintains full responsibility for the staff and their own individual ministries. The Ministry Action Team leaders' involvement does not override the pastor's responsibility for the staff.

The "Model Team"

Obviously, the paid staff must model teamwork and accountability for the lay ministry teams. The design of the above ministry description reflects our desire to work together with the church team leaders.

So what's the bottom line? Our Trinity "ships" (Fellowship, Stewardship, Worship, Friendship, Partnership, Leadership, Discipleship) sail smoothly when our ministry teammates have clearly defined roles and job descriptions. Empowered leaders with a clear understanding of their ministry assignments assist greatly in Kingdom-building!

A Final Word: Don't Quit Holding Hands!

A troop of Boy Scouts gathered for their annual hike in the woods. Taking off at sunrise, they commenced a 15-mile trek through some of the most scenic grounds in the country. About midmorning, the Scouts came across an abandoned section of railroad track. Each, in turn, tried to walk the narrow rails, but after only a few unsteady steps, each lost his balance and tumbled off.

After watching one after another fall off the iron rail, two of the Scouts offered a bet to the rest of the troop. The two bet that they could both walk the entire length of the railroad track without falling off even once.

The other boys laughed and said, "No way!" Challenged to make good their boast, the two boys jumped up on opposite rails, simply reached out and held hands to balance each other, and steadily walked the entire section of track with no difficulty.

The moral of the story is that seemingly impossible tasks are easier when we are willing to work together. To keep from stumbling, we need to reach out to our teammates and never quit holding hands! I realize that some of you will be implementing these changes within the context of a small- or medium-sized church, and the task might seem impossible. But don't despair! I've been there! The best method is to *gradually* begin to make the changes you can make. The other changes will come in time. For example, even if you can initially establish only three Ministry Action Teams, grab the hands of your gifted laypersons and begin walking that "railroad track."

> *We must welcome the future, remembering that soon it will be the past; and we must respect the past, remembering that it was once all that was humanly possible.*
> —George Santayan

Team-Building Tips

- Ask for feedback to be directed to the entire team.
- Take the entire team to a leadership seminar.
- Build an atmosphere that is conducive to open communication.
- Remember, team members will fail.
- Teach the team Eph. 4:11-12.
- Resign as general manager of the universe and let God guide the team!